Federal Budget Policy

Studies of Government Finance

TITLES PUBLISHED

Federal Budget Policy

DAVID J. OTT AND ATTIAT F. OTT

Studies of Government Finance

THE BROOKINGS INSTITUTION

WASHINGTON, D.C.

THE BROOKINGS INSTITUTION is an independent organization devoted to nonpartisan research, education, and publication in economics, government, foreign policy, and the social sciences generally. Its principal purposes are to aid in the development of sound public policies and to promote public understanding of issues of national importance.

The Institution was founded December 8, 1927, to merge the activities of the Institute for Government Research, founded in 1916, the Institute of Economics, founded in 1922, and the Robert Brookings Graduate School of Economics and Government, founded in 1924.

The general administration of the Institution is the responsibility of a self-perpetuating Board of Trustees. The Trustees are likewise charged with maintaining the independence of the staff and fostering the most favorable conditions for creative research and education. The immediate direction of the policies, program, and staff of the Institution is vested in the President, assisted by the division directors and an advisory council, chosen from the professional staff of the Institution.

In publishing a study, the Institution presents it as a competent treatment of a subject worthy of public consideration. The interpretations and conclusions in such publications are those of the author or authors and do not purport to represent the views of the other staff members, officers, or trustees of the Brookings Institution.

Foreword

THIS VOLUME on federal budget policy is part of the Brookings series of Studies of Government Finance, a special program of research and education in taxation and government expenditures at the federal, state, and local levels, sponsored by the National Committee on Government Finance. It is one of two publications in this series that is primarily educational. The other volume is James Maxwell's *Financing State and Local Governments*. The purpose of both these volumes is to present the accumulated knowledge of economists and others about government finances, so that public understanding of these areas may be advanced, the public's perception of issues may be sharpened, and factual and institutional materials may be readily at hand when the issues are publicly discussed.

The federal budget is important to every citizen. It is the basic planning document of the federal government, and at all times it exerts a significant influence on the state of the economy. It is hoped that the present volume will be helpful to the general public and to public officials, as well as to specialists, in understanding the federal budget and in deciding on issues raised in the discussions of public policy that are precipitated by the submission of the budget to the Congress each year.

This study was prepared jointly by David and Attiat Ott, both members of the economics department of Southern Methodist University. The authors received help from many sources. They wish to express their appreciation for critical comments by Leonard A. Silk, Samuel M. Cohn, Otto Eckstein, Marshall A. Robinson, Naomi Sweeney, Charles B. Saunders, Jr., Carl Tiller, and Wilfred Lewis,

Jr. Miss Irene Lurie and Mrs. Sheau-eng Lau acted as research assistants at different stages of the project, and Mrs. Jane Brashares supervised the production of the final draft. The study was edited and indexed by Virginia C. Haaga. Joseph A. Pechman, Director of Economic Studies, provided continuous encouragement and critical comment, without which the volume would not have reached its final form.

The National Committee on Government Finance was established in 1960 by the trustees of the Brookings Institution to supervise a comprehensive program of studies on taxation and government expenditure. The program, sponsored by the National Committee, is supported with funds provided by the Ford Foundation.

The views expressed in this study are those of the authors and do not purport to represent the views of the National Committee on Government Finance or the staff members, officers, or trustees of the Brookings Institution, or the Ford Foundation.

ROBERT D. CALKINS
President

June 1965
The Brookings Institution

Studies of Government Finance

Studies of Government Finance is a special program of research and education in taxation and government expenditures at the federal, state, and local levels. These studies are under the supervision of the National Committee on Government Finance appointed by the trustees of the Brookings Institution, and are supported by a special grant from the Ford Foundation.

MEMBERS OF THE ADVISORY COMMITTEE

Contents

Text Tables

Figures

Appendix Tables

CHAPTER I

Introduction

THIS BOOK IS ABOUT the federal budget, which has amounted to one-fifth of total national output, or Gross National Product, in recent years. Decisions regarding taxes and expenditures affect jobs, the "value of the dollar," the growth of the national economy, and national defense. They bear on the question of government versus private use of resources, federal versus state-local responsibility, and the viability of the private enterprise economy.

Those who make these critical decisions rely on staffs of specialists for guidance as well as on their own knowledge and experience. But the layman, who is ultimately called upon to judge the wisdom of the decisions, too often finds that he lacks the basis for informed judgment. To be informed about budget policy requires some familiarity with budget accounting concepts, the budget process, and the history of federal budget experience. To make informed judgments about federal spending and tax policy, knowledge of what the budget *should* do is also essential. This is true at every level, from the President and his staff, who formulate federal budget policy, to the congressman and the individual citizen, who must have some basis for judging the President's fiscal program.

The purposes of this volume are (1) to explain, as far as possible in nontechnical language, the criteria that most economists would offer to guide decisions about federal spending and taxation; and (2) to provide in one place institutional and descriptive material about the federal budget, federal budgeting history, and how the budget is formulated to help the reader in becoming informed about current budget policies.

The book begins with the factual and descriptive background material. Chapter II explains the differences among three concepts of the federal budget—the administrative, cash, and national income budgets—and the uses and limitations of each. These budgets are often confused in public discussion, and improper deductions result from the confusion. Chapter III tells how the federal budget is made, from the formulation and presentation of the President's budget through congressional consideration and approval, the actual disbursement of funds, and the audit of accounts. It also summarizes past improvements in the budget process and some suggested further changes. In Chapter IV the history of federal finances since 1792 is reviewed briefly, and the outstanding features are discussed. Trends in federal expenditures relative to output, population, and prices, in war-connected and other federal expenditures, and in the composition of federal expenditures are presented. The trend in types of receipts is also discussed and the record of deficits and surpluses shown.

Chapters V through VIII deal with the economics of federal budget policy. The impact of budget policy on the nation's economy is discussed in Chapter V. It explains how tax and expenditure decisions of the federal government affect output, employment, prices, and economic growth and how budget policy can help achieve certain economic goals related to output, employment, prices, and growth. The practical problems involved in using the budget as an instrument to affect the economy are given special attention.

Chapter VI deals with possible alternative budget programs in light of the discussion in Chapter V. The virtues and problems of an annually balanced budget program are compared and contrasted with various other budget programs, such as the stabilizing budget proposal of the CED and the Swedish budget proposals.

If the budget policy of the federal government requires running deficits and increasing the national debt, what will be the results? Is there a burden associated with the national debt? Will increases in the national debt lead to bankruptcy? These and other issues are taken up in Chapter VII.

The final chapter deals with criteria for judging federal spending—both the total amount and by function—apart from the impact of federal spending on output, prices, and employment.

The reader should remember that not only is expenditure and tax policy important, it is very controversial. The budget policy of an administration is often the leading domestic issue in national elections. This increases the need for the public to be informed on the facts and significance of budget decisions, but it also makes more difficult a detached study of budget policy, particularly of the criteria that should guide budget decisions. This volume is not a political tract; at least it was not intended to be one. Its objective is to present the views dominant among professional economists. The ideas and views should stand on their logic and assumptions and not on any political implications they may have.

CHAPTER II

Types of Federal Budgets and Their Uses

IN A DISCUSSION OF federal budget policy, it must be clear which budget is meant. The fiscal activities of the federal government are reported in several ways; there are, in fact, three different budgets compiled to summarize federal fiscal activity. These are: (1) the administrative or conventional budget, (2) the consolidated cash budget, and (3) the national income accounts budget.[1] Each of them meets a different need, but unfortunately they are sometimes confused in newspaper reporting or congressional debate, or when citizens formally or informally discuss and evaluate federal budget policy. In this chapter the three budgets and their uses will be compared so that their differences will be clearly understood in later analyses of budgetary policy.

The Administrative Budget

The administrative budget is the oldest and most generally familiar of the three types of budgets. It is this one that the annual budget message of the President has usually centered on in the

[1] For convenience, these three budgets will be referred to as the administrative, cash, and national income budgets, respectively.

past,[2] that the "Budget" in "Bureau of the Budget" stands for, that congressional committees pore over, and that is voted on (though not as a unit) annually in the Congress. This is the budget that congressmen deplore as "too large" or "too small" and that somehow exercises the citizenry despite its bulk and complexity and the fact that very few of them ever see it. Yet this budget by itself is the least meaningful of the three for analyzing federal fiscal policy—for gauging the impact of federal spending and taxation on employment, economic growth, and the price level.

The administrative budget was implemented, relatively late in federal financial history, in the Budget and Accounting Act of 1921. Before this time, individual executive departments dealt directly with congressional committees on their budgets, and concern was over the smallest details of departmental budgets and not with aggregate outlays and taxes and their composition. There had been a brief attempt at Presidential budgeting when Alexander Hamilton was Washington's Secretary of the Treasury, but from 1789 to 1909 little support for coordinated Executive proposals for expenditure and taxing policy was evident. In large part this reflected the fact that federal revenues, chiefly from customs duties, grew faster than expenditures during most of this period of more than a century.

The end of this era of federal finances and the initial steps toward a coordinated federal budget began with the administration of President Taft. Enlarged federal functions and the Spanish-American War had brought about increases in expenditures that tended to outrun the growth in customs and tariff revenues; there were deficits in ten of the sixteen fiscal years 1894-1909.[3] Concern over the problem and the work of reformers and muckrakers led President Taft to appoint a Commission on Economy and Efficiency in 1910. The Commission Report two years later strongly urged the establishment of a federal budget system, and this was also recommended by President Taft in his letter of transmittal. However, the political situation in 1912 and for several years thereafter prevented congressional action on these recommendations. In 1921, however,

[2] The budget presented in January 1963 shifted emphasis to the cash budget. Before that time the budget message centered attention on the administrative budget.

[3] Jesse M. Burkhead, *Government Budgeting* (John Wiley and Sons, 1956), pp. 16-17.

the Budget and Accounting Act, which incorporated the Commission's proposals, was passed and became law with the signature of President Harding.[4]

The Budget and Accounting Act contained these provisions: (1) the President was directed to prepare annually and submit to the Congress a budget giving complete information on the condition of the Treasury, revenues, and past expenditures and a proposed program of future expenditures and financing; (2) the Bureau of the Budget was created to act as the agent of the President in preparing the budget; and (3) the General Accounting Office, with a Comptroller-General as head, was created to act on behalf of Congress as an independent watchdog over expenditures, taking over the auditing functions and other duties formerly vested in the Comptroller of the Treasury and the six auditors for the departments, whose offices were abolished.

The administrative budget of today is virtually as specified in that 1921 law. The only major change has been to bring wholly owned federal corporations into the federal budget process, which was accomplished by the Corporation Control Act of 1945.

The administrative budget is primarily an instrument of management and control by the Executive and Congress over activities financed with federal funds (largely congressional appropriations). It is the means by which the President quantifies his proposed programs and sends them to Congress for perusal, modification, and approval. The approved budget then becomes a tool of Executive control over the spending of the various departments, agencies, and government corporations.

Table 1 shows the administrative budget for the fiscal year 1965, with receipts listed by type of tax and expenditures broken down by function.[5] Categories of receipts and expenditures are

[4] A predecessor of The Brookings Institution—The Institute for Government Research—was instrumental in educating the public to the need for a national budget system. The first four publications of the Institute dealt with this issue; and its Director, W. F. Willoughby, was a noted authority on the subject, having served as a member of the Commission on Economy and Efficiency. For a discussion of the movement for budgetary reform, see W. F. Willoughby, *The National Budget System* (The Johns Hopkins Press, 1927), Chap. III.

[5] Expenditures may also be classified in other ways. For example, they can be broken down by department or agency or by object of expenditure (paper, salaries, office equipment, etc.).

TABLE 1. United States Government Administrative Budget, Fiscal Year 1965

(In millions of dollars, estimated)[a]

Item	Amount
Receipts	
Individual income taxes	47,000
Corporation income taxes	25,600
Excise taxes	10,733
Estate and gift taxes	2,800
Customs	1,415
Miscellaneous budget receipts	4,485
Interfund transactions	−833
Total receipts	91,200
Expenditures	
National defense	52,160
International affairs and finance	4,043[b]
Space research and technology	4,900
Agriculture and agricultural resources	4,477[b]
Natural resources	2,735
Commerce and transportation	3,372
Housing and community development	−280
Health, labor and welfare	6,208
Education	1,509
Veterans benefits and services	5,383
Interest	11,286
General government	2,417
Allowance for Appalachia	3
Allowance for contingencies	100
Interfund transactions	−833
Total expenditures	97,481
Budget surplus (+) or deficit (−)	−6,281

Source: U. S. Bureau of the Budget, *The Budget of the United States Government, Fiscal Year 1966*, pp. 490–97, hereinafter referred to as *1966 Budget*.

[a] Details may not add to totals due to rounding.

[b] Beginning with 1964, expenditures for the Food for Peace program are included in International Affairs. Prior to this they were included in Agriculture.

generally self-explanatory except for "Interfund transactions." The latter are items that are expenditures of one government agency and receipts of another. For example, the Export-Import Bank of Washington may pay interest (on its capital borrowed from the federal government) to the Treasury. This would be shown as both a receipt of the Treasury and an expenditure of the Export-Import Bank, and to this extent there is double counting. Thus this item is subtracted from *both* receipts and expenditures as an "Interfund transaction."

What are the salient features of the administrative budget? First, and most important, *not all federal receipts and expenditures are included*. Excluded are certain expenditures, such as social security benefits and federal grants to states for highway construction, which are made out of special "trust funds," and certain receipts, notably social security contributions of individuals and certain excise taxes that are earmarked for these funds. These trust fund receipts and expenditures will be about $31 billion in fiscal 1965. They are excluded from the administrative budget because they represent fiduciary activities of the government: the revenues are held in trust for individuals or groups of individuals and do not "belong" to the government; therefore, payments out of the funds are not considered "costs of government" in the usual sense.

A second feature of the administrative budget is that *expenditures and receipts are generally recorded on a cash basis,* that is, on the date of actual receipt or payment rather than on the date the obligation arises. Interest expense, however, is on an accrual basis.

Third, the *receipts and outlays of government enterprises included in the administrative budget are solely for enterprises that are wholly owned by the federal government,* and they are represented by a net figure entered only on the expenditure side. For example, the operations of the Post Office Department are classified as "postal service" under "commerce and transportation" in Table 1, but the figure entered represents the *net* expenditure of that department, or the difference between its gross receipts and its expenditures. Data on federal government-sponsored (but not wholly owned) enterprises, such as the Federal Deposit Insurance Corporation, are not included at all, except when the federal government buys their securities or receives interest from them.

The Consolidated-Cash Budget

The administrative budget was a fairly good representation of federal government receipts and expenditures until the late 1930's. However, with the establishment and growth of various trust funds, such as the Old Age and Survivors' Insurance, Disability Insurance, and Unemployment Insurance trust funds, and the growth of government-sponsored enterprises, increasingly significant amounts of federal receipts and expenditures were excluded from the detailed budget review process and from the administrative budget. It became obvious that the administrative budget no longer presented an accurate picture of federal fiscal activity or of the impact of government taxation and spending on the economy.

Research within the Division of Research and Statistics of the Federal Reserve Board[6] thus produced the concept of the consolidated-cash budget to provide a measure of federal cash payments to, and receipts from, the "public"—all non-federal-government economic units. The cash budget is useful in picturing *total* receipts and expenditures during a given period; it shows the cash inflows and outflows of the federal government and its financial position much better than does the administrative budget.

To derive the cash budget from administrative budget figures, three basic adjustments are made: (1) receipts and expenditures of federal trust funds and federal government-sponsored enterprises are added; (2) some intragovernmental transactions among accounts of the administrative budget, trust funds, and government-sponsored enterprises are excluded, since they do not represent transactions with the public; and (3) a few budget and trust account transactions are adjusted to a cash basis. The details of these adjustments are explained in Appendix C.

The difference between the receipts and expenditures in the cash budget and in the administrative budget is clear from the comparison in Table 2. The administrative budget is some $26 billion lower on the receipts side and $24 billion lower on the expenditures side.

There is also a difference in deficits: the administrative budget shows a deficit of $6,281 million and the cash budget a deficit of $4,009 million. This reflects the adjustments made in receipts and expenditures. As Table 3 shows, the lower deficit in the cash budget reflects primarily the surplus in the trust accounts; the effect of the other adjustments is small.

The deficit or surplus in the cash budget represents the net impact of federal spending and taxation on the assets of the public. A deficit in the cash budget shows that the public is accumulating

[6] See Lewis H. Kimmel, *Federal Budget and Fiscal Policy 1789-1958* (Brookings Institution, 1959), pp. 322-24.

**TABLE 2. Receipts from and Payments to the Public (The Cash Budget)'
Fiscal Year 1965**

(In millions of dollars, estimated)[a]

Item	Amount
Receipts from the public	
Administrative budget receipts (Table 1)	91,200
Trust fund receipts (Table C-1)	30,515
Less:	
Intragovernmental transactions (Table C-2)	4,234
Exercise of monetary authority (Appendix C)	97
Total, receipts from the public	117,384
Payments to the public	
Administrative budget expenditures (Table 1)	97,481
Trust fund expenditures (Table C-1)	29,045
Less:	
Intragovernmental transactions (Table C-2)	4,234
Debt issuance in lieu of checks, net (Table C-3)	1,119
Changes in outstanding checks (Appendix C)	−200
Total, payments to the public	121,393
Cash budget surplus (+) or deficit (−)	−4,009

Source: *1966 Budget*, pp. 356–65, 492, 496–98.
[a] Details may not add to totals due to rounding.

government securities or cash: either the government is issuing debt
to cover the deficit that the public is accumulating, or it is running
down its cash balances, which are then transferred to the public.
The deficit in the cash budget equals the net accumulation by the
public of government debt and money due to federal fiscal action.

**TABLE 3. Factors Producing Differences in Surplus or Deficit Between
Cash and Administrative Budgets, Fiscal Year 1965**

(In millions of dollars, estimated)

Item	Amount
Surplus (+) or deficit (−) in administrative budget	−6,281
Plus:	
Surplus of trust funds	1,470
Other adjustments (See Appendix A)	802
Surplus (+) or deficit (−) in cash budget	−4,009

Source: Derived from Tables 1 and 2.

The National Income Accounts Budget

As has been seen, the cash budget is a much more meaningful indicator of the size and scope of federal activity than is the administrative budget. It furnishes comprehensive totals of cash transactions and is thus especially valuable for determining government financing and net borrowing requirements, and the way in which this government financing will affect the cash and financial assets of the public. In short, the cash budget is useful for analyzing the *financial* impact of the government's overall program.

The *national income budget* serves another purpose: it is the best measure of the *economic* impact of federal taxing and spending policies during any period of time.

The national income budget differs somewhat from the administrative and cash budgets because it has to correspond in concept to the system followed in the national income accounts, a system of dual-entry accounts used by the Department of Commerce to estimate the current productive activity of residents of the United States. On the one hand, the accounts show the market values of the currently produced output of goods and services, classified by type of expenditure: (1) consumer expenditures, (2) gross private expenditures on equipment, new construction, and inventories, (3) federal, state, and local government purchases of goods and services, and (4) net exports. The total of these items is called Gross National Product (GNP). On the other hand, the accounts measure and classify the stream of income generated in the process of producing GNP: for example, wages and salaries, professional income, rental income, corporate profits, interest, and others.

The national income budget differs from the cash budget with respect to (1) coverage, (2) netting and consolidation, (3) timing of receipts and expenditures, and (4) the exclusion of capital transactions.

The national income budget does not cover receipts and expenditures of the District of Columbia, which it classifies as part of the state and local sector instead of the federal sector. As for netting and consolidation, interest payments and government purchases are put on a net basis, and some items are added to both receipts and expenditures, in particular employer and employee contributions to

TABLE 4. Derivation of the National Income Budget from the Cash Budget, Fiscal Year 1965

(In billions of dollars, estimated)

Item	Receipts	Expenditures
Cash budget	117.4	121.4
Coverage		
Less: District of Columbia	0.3	0.4
Netting and consolidation		
Less: Interest and related earnings	1.9	1.9
Plus: Contributions to federal employees' retirement funds, etc.	2.1	2.1
Timing		
Plus: Excess of corporate tax accruals over collections, personal taxes, etc.	−0.9	
Plus: Excess of interest accruals over payments, excess of deliveries over expenditures and other items		2.5
Less: Commodity Credit Corporation foreign currency exchanges		0.8
Capital transactions		
Less: Realization upon loans and investments, sale of government property, etc.	0.4	
Less: Loans, FNMA secondary market mortgage purchases, redemption of IMF notes, etc.		1.4
Less: Purchase of land and existing assets, and other items		0.5
National income budget	116.0	121.0

Source: *1966 Budget*, p. 357.

federal employee retirement funds.[7] Neither of these adjustments, it should be noted, affects the size of the deficit or surplus, since receipts and expenditures are changed equally. The timing adjustments basically involve putting receipts (other than withheld income taxes) on an accrual basis, rather than on an "as collected" basis, and putting expenditures on a "goods delivery date" basis rather than on a cash payment basis. The capital transactions adjustments exclude expenditures on existing assets and loans (or loan repayments), since these expenditures are not on *currently produced* goods and services.[8]

[7] These contributions are excluded as an intragovernmental transaction in the cash budget, but in national income accounting they are considered to be part of the total compensation of governmental employees.

[8] It should be noted that the capital transactions excluded from the national income budget *do* reflect federal fiscal activity. Therefore, the national income budget is not a comprehensive measure of federal fiscal activity. A more detailed discussion of the timing and capital transactions adjustments is presented in Appendix D.

FIGURE I. Federal Deficits and Surpluses Under Three Budget Concepts, 1948–64

(In billions of dollars)

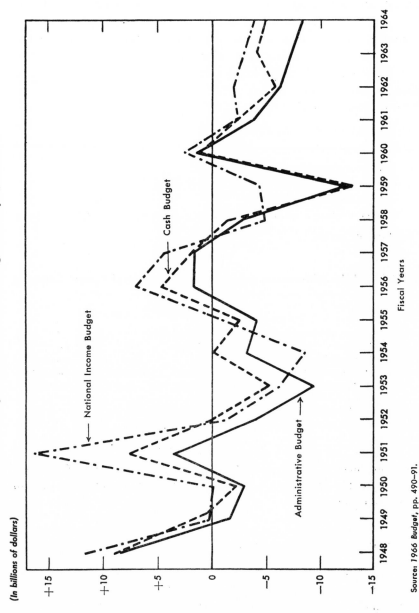

Source: *1966 Budget,* pp. 490–91.

The effect of all these adjustments on receipts and expenditures in the national income budget is shown for the fiscal year 1965 in Table 4. It can be seen that the total magnitude of these adjustments is nowhere near as great as that involved in obtaining the cash budget from the administrative budget.

The major differences among the three budgets as to the treatment of expenditures and receipts can be conveniently assigned to four general categories:

1. Timing of receipts
2. Timing of expenditures
3. Treatment of credit transactions
4. Treatment of trust fund transactions

Table 5 shows how the three budgets generally differ in these three major areas:

TABLE 5. Major Differences Among the Three Federal Budget Concepts

Item	Administrative	Cash	National Income
Timing of receipts	Cash basis	Cash	Accrual
Timing of expenditures	Cash	Cash	Delivery
Treatment of credit transactions	Included	Included	Excluded
Treatment of trust fund transactions	Excluded	Included	Included

Source: Adapted from *Economic Report of the President* (January 1962), p. 78.

Figure I on page 13 shows how the differences affect the deficits and surpluses in the three budgets for fiscal years 1948-64. In most years the size of the deficit or surplus differed considerably among the three budgets.

Summary and Conclusion

This chapter has emphasized the differences among the administrative, cash, and national income versions of the federal budget, differences that result from the different purposes for which each budget is intended.

The *administrative budget* is primarily an instrument of management and control of those federal activities that are financed with what are considered to be federally owned funds, mainly through annual congressional appropriations. Therefore, it does not account for the expenditures and receipts of the trust funds—social security, highway, and others—and those of government-sponsored enterprises, which are financed from special taxes or receipts and not from federally owned funds.

The *cash budget* includes receipts and expenditures of the trust funds and government-sponsored enterprises, since its purpose is to measure cash payments to, and receipts from, the public and the resulting effect on the assets of the public stemming from federal fiscal activity.

The *national accounts budget,* designed to measure the federal contribution to total economic activity (output) of the nation, excludes some purely financial credit transactions that are included as receipts or expenditures in the other two budgets. It generally accounts for receipts or expenditures when they have their economic impact, which is not necessarily when the federal government receives cash or pays it out.

Because of these differences in the three budgets, expenditures, receipts, and the surplus or deficit may be quite different in each as measured for any period.[9] None of these figures can be considered *the* right one. The proper budget depends on the problem under consideration. Economic analysis, however, usually requires either the cash budget or the national income budget.[10]

[9] None of the budget statements directly reflects government guarantees and insurance activities, unless losses result from such activities. Comparisons over time are misleading if there is a shift from direct-loan programs, which are included (with net amounts) in the budget, to guarantee programs, which are not included. *See* Gerhard Colm, *The Federal Budget and the National Economy,* Planning Pamphlet No. 90 (National Planning Association, March 1955), pp. 12-13.

[10] It has been suggested that the federal government should distinguish between *current* expenditures and *capital* expenditures (the latter involves the acquisition of assets by the federal government, while the former does not) and that receipts should also be divided into those on "capital account" and those on "current account." This procedure has been followed by Sweden and Denmark. The United States budget document regularly contains a special analysis (D), which presents the capital components of budget expenditures. For a discussion of capital budgeting, *see* Colm, *op. cit.,* pp. 86-94.

CHAPTER III

The Budget Process

CRUCIAL TO ANY discussion of budget policy—setting the levels and composition of taxes and expenditures to achieve certain goals —is a knowledge of the administrative and political process through which expenditures and taxes are, in fact, determined. This chapter describes the process at the federal level and also indicates briefly the pressures, forces, and individuals involved in making the many difficult decisions that go into the final budget product.

Although budgeting is a continuing process, the term "budget cycle" is often used to emphasize its periodicity. There are clearly defined phases of budgeting in most budgetary systems. At the federal level in the United States, four phases can be identified: (1) Executive preparation and submission, (2) legislative authorization and appropriation, (3) execution, and (4) audit.

Executive Preparation and Submission

Every year the Executive Branch of the federal government prepares both an administrative and a cash budget, which in January are submitted to the Congress by the President with his Budget Message. These budgets are for the fiscal years beginning on the first of July following transmittal of the Budget Message. However, preparation of these budgets begins long before January. Figure II shows the approximate time sequence of, and participants in, each stage of budget preparation by the Executive Branch. The timing suggested is only approximate and may be different under various pressures or in the case of specific departments. Nevertheless, the chart does indicate the lead time required in preparing the Executive's budget.

Figure II also illustrates a basic characteristic of budgeting in the Executive Branch—the two-way flow of decisions, up from the departments and agencies and then back down from the Bureau of the Budget and the President.[1] The individual organizational units in the departments and agencies make early plans for their programs and expenditures, which are consolidated and reviewed by the budget offices in each agency. These provide the agency with information when, in May and June, probable requirements for the coming year are discussed with the Bureau of the Budget. The Bureau then can advise the President as to preliminary agency and department plans and goals. This information, together with projections of the economic outlook and revenue estimates from the Treasury, the Bureau of the Budget, and the Council of Economic Advisers (in June, July, or August), gives the President and his advisers the basis for tentative overall budget policy decisions—as to total expenditures, revenues, and programs. Guidelines reflecting these policy decisions then flow back down, through the Bureau of the Budget, to the departments and agencies in the form of planning figures to guide the preparation of their eventual budget submissions in the Fall. They must then either modify their programs to fit the guidelines or appeal to the Bureau of the Budget and possibly even to the Executive for a reversal of the decision affecting their budgets.

[1] It should be noted that the budget of the Department of Defense is handled somewhat differently from those of other agencies. The Bureau of the Budget participates with the financial officers of the Defense Department in a review of the requests of the various services for budgetary allowances, but its role here is not quite the same as with other agencies. It acts more as an adviser to the Secretary of Defense than as an arbiter; more decisions here must be taken for Presidential action. Also final Defense budgetary decisions are made later than those of other agencies; many of the crucial ones are held until late December.

FIGURE II. Formulation of the Executive Budget

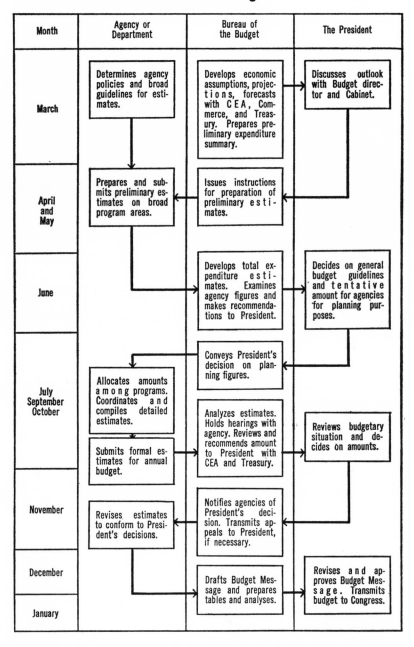

Month	Agency or Department	Bureau of the Budget	The President
March	Determines agency policies and broad guidelines for estimates.	Develops economic assumptions, projections, forecasts with C E A, Commerce, and Treasury. Prepares preliminary expenditure summary.	Discusses outlook with Budget director and Cabinet.
April and May	Prepares and submits preliminary estimates on broad program areas.	Issues instructions for preparation of preliminary estimates.	
June		Develops total expenditure estimates. Examines agency figures and makes recommendations to President.	Decides on general budget guidelines and tentative amount for agencies for planning purposes.
July September October	Allocates amounts among programs. Coordinates and compiles detailed estimates.	Conveys President's decision on planning figures.	
	Submits formal estimates for annual budget.	Analyzes estimates. Holds hearings with agency. Reviews and recommends amount to President with CEA and Treasury.	Reviews budgetary situation and decides on amounts.
November	Revises estimates to conform to President's decisions.	Notifies agencies of President's decision. Transmits appeals to President, if necessary.	
December January		Drafts Budget Message and prepares tables and analyses.	Revises and approves Budget Message. Transmits budget to Congress.

18

Agency Budgeting

The first step in this two-way flow of decisions is agency budgeting. All federal agencies and departments have budget offices and officers. The organization of these offices may vary, but generally the budget officer serves as a member of the department or agency staff. Through the agency budgeting office flows the information on programs and costs which enables the administrator to decide on programs and expenditures to be proposed. The "line agencies," within their legal limits, are usually encouraged to submit all their plans and proposals so that adequate information will be available for a final decision.

Program and expenditure decisions are necessarily made on the basis of a broad range of criteria, from cost-benefit calculations to the political demand for a certain government service. However, the decision-making process has a better foundation than this statement implies. The bulk of expenditure and program decisions in most agencies is marginal. That is, the decisions relate to changes in expenditures for existing programs. Further, a large segment of budget expenditures is virtually outside the budget process. For the last few years such items as interest on the public debt, veterans' pensions, and agricultural price supports have accounted for over 60 percent of total nondefense budget expenses and for over 25 percent of total budget expenditures. The levels of expenditure for these items are determined by provisions written into legislation authorizing the programs and by other factors not readily subject to annual budgetary control. They are, however, subject to review, and occasionally legislation is proposed to change them. The crucial budget decisions, then, relate primarily to programs subject to budgetary control and take the form of an evaluation of relatively small increases or decreases in costs and activities.

Agencies and their "line people" are expected to be advocates of increased appropriations. It is generally accepted as natural and inevitable by Congress and the Budget Bureau that agency budget offices will have a strong interest in justifying their appropriation requests. After all, they are expected to believe in their work and be enthusiastic about it. In fact, Congress and the Bureau of the Budget would find their task much more difficult if the agencies refused to play the role of advocate; in the advocacy role the agencies pro-

vide information crucial to congressional and Budget Bureau decisions—information Congress and the Bureau would otherwise have
to obtain for themselves.

On the other hand, agencies or departments rarely ask for *all*
they feel they could use. If they did, the Bureau of the Budget or
Congress would probably make substantial cuts; to have proposals
cut sharply every year would set a precedent for the future. In any
case, some cuts can be expected in an agency budget. As guardians
of the public purse, the Budget Bureau and Congress are expected
to be more economy-minded than agency heads, who are responsible
for the execution of specific programs.

Given the fact that agencies cannot, for strategic reasons, aim
too high or too low, how do they decide just where to aim? They do
it by seeking out and receiving clues and hints from the Executive
Branch, Congress, clientele groups, and their own organizations.
They are able in most cases to get a rough idea of what will prove
acceptable to the Budget Bureau, the President and his advisers,
and the appropriations subcommittees in Congress.

As Figure II shows, agencies and their line divisions begin
building the budget sixteen months prior to the start of the fiscal
year for which it is intended.[2] The process starts with the "budget
call" by the agency budget office, which outlines policy decisions
that have been made and transmits the necessary technical information regarding forms and reports by the reporting units. By May
most agency budget officers are in a position to consolidate field requests and to confer with the Budget Bureau. During May and June
the agencies discuss plans and probable requirements with the Bureau, and both thus get an idea of the needs and problems and the
restraints required.

The Policy Letter

At this point, the budget process is centered in the Bureau of
the Budget, the central budgeting office. In June the Bureau begins
to put together the pieces that form the overall budget for the next
fiscal year. In addition to the information provided by the agencies,
the Bureau consults with the Council of Economic Advisers and the

[2] Actually preparation of the budget begins even earlier. The Bureau of the
Budget now engages in some long-range (multi-year) planning. Preliminary plans
and policies are developed each Spring for the budget for the fiscal year beginning twenty-seven months later. Thus budgeting each year often takes as a
starting point the projections developed a year earlier.

Treasury Department on the economic outlook and related revenue estimates. Concurrently the Director of the Bureau and his staff, together with the Council of Economic Advisers and the Treasury, deal directly with the President and his advisers on emerging problems, initial clearance on major program decisions, and the overall revenue and expenditure outlook. Thus the administration's overall budget policy for the forthcoming fiscal year begins to take shape.

Next comes a meeting of the Director with each of the major agency heads to discuss the economic outlook, revenue, the total budget picture, the President's overall budget objective, and the agency's major budget items. After these meetings and further discussions with the President, a "policy letter" is usually sent by the Director of the Bureau of the Budget to agency and department heads, giving information on various policy aims. More important, the general budget policy formulated in discussions with administration policy-workers is translated into budget planning figures for some twenty agencies. These are not ceiling figures. Rather, the Bureau is saying that in view of the administration's program, it is likely that the agency's budget will be somewhere near the planning figure. Agencies can bring in estimates exceeding the planning figure, but if they do, they must indicate where they plan cuts if they are required to get back down to the planning figure.

Call for Estimates

The "flow-back" to the agencies and departments is also reflected in the "call for estimates," usually issued in July or August also. This document notifies the agencies and departments of the planned time schedule, the forms to be used, and suggestions for reports and materials to accompany each budget.

This is a crucial stage in the budget process. The agencies and departments conduct intensive examinations of their budgets in light of the planning figures or budget directives that have been passed down to them and in light of the previous year's action by the Appropriations Committees of Congress. The agency or department that is well within its planning figure has no problems. (This is so rare as to be a unique experience in the career of an agency budget officer.) On the other hand, most face a difficult decision as to where to cut (in the absence of specific directives), or whether to cut at all or to fight it out by appeal to the Budget Bureau and, if necessary, the President himself.

Review by Bureau of the Budget

The departmental estimates, when formulated, are then submitted to the Bureau of the Budget, usually sometime after September 30. They are reviewed by examiners of the Bureau, and then hearings are held, first with the agency official and then within the Bureau, where the final decisions on Bureau recommendations to the President are made. At these hearings the department or agency presents and defends its budget before the examiner and other staff members of the Budget Bureau.

Relations between agencies and the Budget Bureau are important at this stage, in particular the relation between the agency and the Bureau's examiners assigned to it. On the one hand, the agency is reluctant to incur Budget Bureau disfavor, for the Bureau's recommendations to the President do carry weight. Congress usually exceeds the President's appropriations recommendations only with some reluctance, and more commonly cuts them. At the same time, the Bureau cannot restrain the agencies too much, for "end-runs" by agencies to Congress to get funds disapproved by the Bureau are not unusual. So both parties are constrained, and the end result is usually somewhere between what each would prefer.

Based on the hearings and his knowledge of agency programs and operations and overall policies, the Budget Bureau examiner submits his recommendations to the Director of the Bureau, usually after informal consultation with the Bureau staff. At this stage, the examiner's recommendations are subjected to a relatively formal evaluation by the Bureau of the Budget, which is called the "Director's review." This is conducted by top staff members of the Bureau —the Director, the Deputy Director, and other officials, with the Director usually serving as chairman.

Presidential Review

Concurrently with the Director's review, the last stage of Executive budget preparation is being conducted—Presidential review of the budget as it emerges from the Bureau and preparation of the annual budget document. After the President's review, his approved "allowances" are sent to each agency head, who then may accept them or appeal to the Bureau, to the White House, or to the President himself, and sometimes thus obtain another hearing on some of the issues. Also at this very hectic time, final conclusions are drawn concerning the economic outlook and prospective revenue, and these, together with the emerging expenditure estimates of the Bureau, make it possible for the Bureau, the Council of Economic Advisers, and the Treasury to recommend last-minute changes that will affect the size of the budget surplus or deficit. Also at this time departments and agencies make final appeals on decisions affecting their budgets.

Somewhat miraculously, considering the coordination and effort involved, the budget document and message are readied and transmitted to Congress, always during the third week in each January.

Congressional Authorization

The distinctive feature of the congressional phase of the budget process in the United States is that expenditures and taxes are considered separately and are the concern of different committees; there is almost no consideration of the administration's budget as a unified proposal. As a matter of fact, the legislative phase of budgeting is usually thought of only in terms of appropriations; taxation is usually viewed as a separate problem from "budget" (appropriation) considerations.

Terminology

Before the process by which the Congress affects the level of expenditures is discussed, the meaning of the terms "expenditures," "authorization," and "appropriation" must be clarified.

The budget document sets forth the President's proposals for the Executive agencies regarding cash expenditures and new obligational authority during a fiscal year. The expenditures Congress finally approves reflect two separate stages of decision. First it must approve the functions for which expenditures are to be made; this is called "authorization." That is, the Congress passes legislation authorizing specific activities, such as foreign aid, defense, etc., but does not provide funds and sometimes does not even specify the amount of funds implied in the activity.[3] As a matter of custom, authorizing legislation must have been enacted before funds are

---

[3] Authorizing legislation now specifies a maximum amount for 30 percent of total funds in the administrative budget.

granted; the provision of funds is considered separately by the Congress.

Funds are provided in *appropriations*—legislation by Congress permitting a government agency or department to commit or obligate the government to certain expenditures, or what is commonly called "new obligational authority."[4] Appropriations come in several forms, ranging from "one-year appropriations," which allow an agency to incur obligations only during one fiscal year (the most common form) to "no-year appropriations," which are available (for obligation and expenditure) until the purpose of the spending is accomplished. Generally, if the obligational authority is not used during the specified period, it "lapses" and is no longer available to the agency unless the Congress specifically reappropriates it.

Expenditures out of new obligational authority need not occur within the period during which the obligation must be "used up." Even in the case of one-year appropriations, where the obligation must be made within the year, the agency is given two more years to pay the bills (after deliveries have been made, etc.).

Since new obligational authority may be granted for a period longer than the fiscal year, there is always a substantial carry-over of obligational authority from previous years. There is also a carry-over of unspent obligations from the previous year or two, that is, obligational authority that has been committed, but under which no expenditures have actually been made. Thus the expenditure totals in a budget reflect expenditures expected to be made during the coming fiscal year out of uncommitted obligational authority—as well as unspent obligations—carried over from previous years, and out of new obligational authority requested in the budget, as is shown in Figure III. Obligational authority and unspent obligations carried over from previous years were estimated to be $169.4 billion as of July 1, 1965. The 1966 budget requested $140.9 billion of new obligational authority, making a total of $310.3 billion available to the agencies. Of this, some $132.5 billion was estimat-

---

[4] Obligational authority is also provided in two other forms: (1) authorizations to expend from debt receipts and (2) contract authorizations. However, these account for only a very small proportion of new obligational authority, and will not be discussed separately here. See U.S. Bureau of the Budget, *The Budget of the United States Government, Fiscal Year 1962*, p. 114, and U.S. Congress, Joint Economic Committee, *The Federal Budget As an Economic Document*, 87 Cong. 2 sess. (1962), pp. 8-13.

FIGURE III. 1966 Expenditures Related to Obligational Authority (Estimated)

(Total Obligational Authority Available—$310.3 billion)

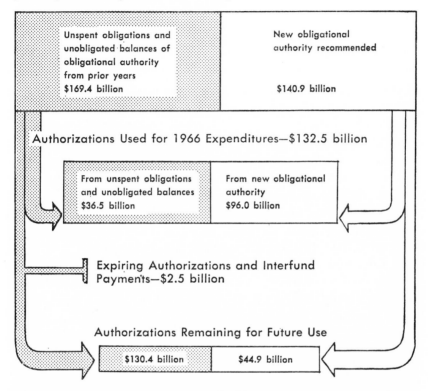

Source: *1966 Budget*. Note that expenditures here of $132.5 billion are larger than total cash expenditures of $121.4 billion. The difference is that no adjustment for intergovernment receipts and expenditures, debt issue in lieu of checks, or changes in outstanding checks has been made.

ed to result in expenditures during the fiscal year 1966, $36.5 billion from unspent obligations and unused obligational authority carried over and $96.0 billion from new obligational authority. With $2.5 billion of expiring authorizations and interfund payments, this would leave about $175.3 billion of obligational authority and unspent obligations for years after fiscal 1966.

In appropriations legislation, then, new obligational authority for the coming fiscal year is determined. Congress does not vote on expenditures by department or agency for the next fiscal year; it only determines new obligational authority. In fact, the effect that congressional changes in the amounts of new obligational authority requested by the President will have on *expenditures* in the next fiscal year is not considered in the debate on appropriations bills.

Congressional Consideration of Appropriations

Tax legislation may be initiated only by the House, and in practice, it has been customary for the House also to initiate appropriations legislation. The Senate has typically acted later and has assumed the role of a liberal counterweight to generally conservative appropriation action by the House.[5]

In the House the content of appropriations measures generally reflects the decisions of the House Committee on Appropriations, and, more specifically, of its various subcommittees. The Appropriations Committee has fifty members—thirty from the majority and twenty from the minority. Its work is done largely in thirteen subcommittees of from five to eleven members each. Each subcommittee is responsible for reporting out one or more appropriations bills, of which there are thirteen or fourteen in each congressional session.

Tremendous power and authority rest with the various subcommittees and their chairmen. Each subcommittee holds hearings on requests from the specific agencies for obligational authority. The hearings have been closed to the public for many years, but a record of what is said is taken and usually printed, except for those portions that relate to national security, which are kept off the record. Testimony is generally confined to agency and bureau heads and their budget officers.[6] After the hearings the subcommittee goes into executive session and decides on appropriations and restrictions on activities to be recommended. The recommendations are usually accompanied by reasons for the action and by comments on the agency's programs, efficiency, and personnel.

The subcommittee's recommendations and report are then sent

[5] In 1962 an open dispute broke out between the House and Senate over initiating appropriations legislation. The House felt that it alone could originate such legislation, but the Senate disagreed. Other issues, such as where Senate-House Conference Committees on appropriations should meet, were also involved. This dispute over powers of origination was not resolved, but the House has continued to originate such legislation.

[6] This is because usually no one else asks to be heard. Subcommittees hear witnesses advocating specific expenditure changes if they come forward.

to the full committee for action. They are rarely discussed or even studied in detail; the full committee almost automatically approves the recommendations of the subcommittee and sends them on to the House as a bill, where they are debated with the House sitting as a Committee of the Whole. On the floor the chairman of the subcommittee acts as floor manager; extended debate is rare, and the bill usually passes expeditiously.[7]

Formerly the Senate did not begin hearings on an appropriations bill until the House bill at least neared passage. Now, however, the Senate sometimes begins hearings on the same subject even before the House bill is written. There, also, the initial work is done in the Appropriations Committee; and, also as in the House, the subcommittees of the Senate Appropriations Committee (of which there are twelve) are really the operating units. They hold hearings, "mark up" the bill, and send it to the full committee, as is done in the House; and here too the recommendations of the subcommittees are almost always accepted by the full committee.

When holding hearings, the Senate subcommittees formerly often resembled courts of appeal. Agencies and departments often relied on the Senate to restore cuts made by the House. This is not as common now as it used to be. Since the Senate began holding some of its hearings before the writing of the House bill, the aura of an appeals court is less evident. Still, after the House has passed, or at least written, its bill, senatorial questioning tends to center on differences between the amounts of obligational authority recommended in the President's budget (or those currently being requested by the agency witnesses), and the amounts granted by the House. More often than not, the Senate subcommittees restore portions of cuts made in the House.

On the floor of the Senate, debate is more extensive on appropriations measures than in the House because of the privilege of free debate. The Senate as a whole tends to be more liberal in appropriations than the House; the final Senate version of appropriations bills is typically higher than that of the House.

Senate-House differences on appropriations are reconciled by a conference committee, which seeks to reach a figure between that

[7] See Jesse Burkhead, *Government Budgeting* (John Wiley and Sons, 1956), pp. 98-99.

agreed on by the two houses—one that the conferees can recommend to their parent bodies. The conference committee draft is returned to the House and Senate for further consideration. Usually it is accepted, but occasionally one or the other house rejects it and sends it back to conference.

After final congressional approval the measure is then sent to the President for his signature or veto. Agencies and departments concerned are consulted where there is a question of possible veto, but appropriations bills are rarely vetoed. The bill must be accepted or rejected as a whole; item veto is not provided for by the Constitution. If the President does not like the bill he usually signs it, but expresses disapproval of certain portions of it. A veto of the whole bill might endanger the acceptable portions the next time through Congress. Where appropriations are considered by the Executive to be too low, it can request changes in the next budget after rounding up additional supporting evidence and mobilizing the force of public opinion. Where unwanted funds are voted, the President can refuse to spend them, though this is rare and somewhat difficult to do.

After all the appropriations measures are passed, in September or October of each year the Budget Bureau prepares the "Midyear Review," which summarizes the final data on appropriations and expenditures resulting from congressional action and updates the revenue estimates of the original budget.

Execution of the Budget

How does the obligational authority granted by Congress to an agency or department get converted into cash expenditures?

Apportionment and Allotment

When the appropriations bill is enacted, an appropriations warrant, drawn by the Treasury and countersigned by the General Accounting Office, is sent to the agency. The agency then reviews and revises its budget in light of the appropriations bill and submits to the Bureau of the Budget a request for apportionment, either by May 21 or within fifteen days of the appropriations bill's passage. Apportionment basically means determining the rate at which the obligational authority can be used—the authority is usually apportioned by quarters over the period in which it is to be used, both to insure that the obligational authority is not used up so fast that the agency finds that it has overspent or that it moved faster than Congress intended and therefore needs more money, and to insure the most economical and effective use of the funds.

The Bureau of the Budget approves or revises the agency apportionment request; in effect, the Bureau is the apportioning authority. This power of apportionment gives the Executive some latitude in controlling the direction and timing of federal obligations incurred, and it has on occasion been used in an effort to accelerate the rate of federal obligation use during recession or to refuse to use funds appropriated by Congress for programs the Executive disapproves.[8]

Within the individual agencies, the use of the obligational authority apportioned by the Bureau is controlled through a similar device. Breaking down the apportionment by organizational unit is called *allotment*.

Obligations Incurred and Expenditures

With but minor exceptions[9] the various agencies actually incur obligations after apportionment by the Bureau of the Budget. Incurring obligations, however, does not necessarily mean immediate cash expenditures. In some cases, the expenditure of funds by an agency virtually coincides with the incurring of obligations; in others, the actual expenditure of funds may lag considerably behind the obligation of funds.

In two cases the time lag between obligations and expenditures is very short. Expenditures for the purchase of existing assets (except land, where the lag may be considerable), for social security benefits, veterans' pensions, public assistance grants to states, unemployment compensation, some farm subsidies, and others involving no use of productive resources typically coincide with, or are very

[8] See *Federal Fiscal Behavior During the Recession of 1957-58,* Bureau of the Budget Staff Report; Statements of Walter W. Heller and David E. Bell in *Hearings before the Joint Economic Committee,* U.S. Congress, 87 Cong. 1 sess. (1961); and *Economic Report of the President* (1962).

[9] See Joint Economic Committee, *The Federal Budget As an Economic Document,* p. 14.

close to, the obligation or commitment. In addition, government expenditures involving the direct employment of resources (in particular the services of government employees) typically occur close to the time of the obligation.

But when the federal government has the private sector employ resources on its behalf, that is, when the federal government buys goods and services produced by the private sector, the lag of expenditures behind obligations may be substantial. This lag is both administrative and technological; it takes private producers time to draw plans, negotiate subcontracts, and deliver the product.[10] This means, in effect, that some of the economic impact on the private sector of government purchases of goods or services occurs long before expenditures or actual delivery of goods. Private producers employ resources and produce goods before they are delivered to the government and payment is made.[11]

Expenditures

When they occur, expenditures are generally made out of Treasury deposits at the twelve Federal Reserve Banks, which are part of the "Account of the Treasurer of the United States." This consists mostly of these Treasury checking accounts at the twelve Federal Reserve Banks and at commercial banks. Federal disbursing officers make payment by issuing checks against the Federal Reserve Bank accounts on the basis of vouchers approved by certifying officers of the various agencies; the amount that can be issued is set by the agency's obligational authority and the apportionment of it by the Bureau of the Budget. These checks are usually deposited in commercial banks, which then receive a credit to their Federal Reserve Bank accounts. The Federal Reserve Bank charges the Treas-

---

[10] See Joint Economic Committee, *The Federal Budget As an Economic Document*, pp. 18-21, and Murray Weidenbaum, "The Federal Government Spending Process," in U.S. Congress, Joint Economic Committee, *Federal Expenditure Policy for Economic Growth and Stability*, 85 Cong. 1 sess. Committee print (1957), p. A35. To the extent that there are progress payments or advance payments, the time lag is reduced. It should be noted that the lag is not as significant in cases where the government is buying goods available for general sale to the private sector. These may be quickly available from inventories of producers. The lag is much more significant for goods produced to the government's specific order.

[11] See Weidenbaum, *op. cit.*, for a discussion of this point.

ury account with the amount of the check and sends it to the Treasury, where checks cashed are verified against the record of checks issued by the disbursing officers.

It is the Treasury's responsibility to maintain working balances at the Federal Reserve Banks that are adequate to meet payments as they occur. For this purpose, amounts are funneled by the Treasury into Federal Reserve accounts from deposits at commercial banks made directly by district officers of the Internal Revenue Service, and from receipts from debt issues.

Audit

The individual agencies and departments are responsible for insuring that the obligations they incur, and the resulting expenditures, are legal with respect to authorizing and appropriations legislation. The Congress, however, receives an independent check through the General Accounting Office, which is headed by the Comptroller General. The GAO "closes the books" of the administrative officers responsible for the custody and use of public funds. It has also played an important role in supervising the accounting systems used by agencies and departments and in insuring that agency reporting results in full disclosure of the receipt and use of funds.

Three major types of audits are made by GAO. Recently the *comprehensive audit* has become the most important. This audit lays stress on the accounting and reporting system and checks transactions selectively. The *general audit* examines the accounts of agency disbursing and certifying officers to determine the legality of each transaction. If illegal or improper handling of receipts or expenditures is discovered, recovery procedures are instituted against responsible officers. The *commercial audit* is applied to government corporations and enterprises. No recovery is possible in this case, but Congress is informed of questionable or improper practices.

The results of GAO audits are transmitted to Congress by the Comptroller General. The results of special investigations of particular agencies by GAO and the annual report are referred to the House and Senate Committees on Government Operations.

Improvements in the Budget Process

Budget procedures and the budget process described in this chapter reflect a number of improvements made in the last twenty years or so, most of them in the Executive phase of the budget.

Changes in the Budget Document

First, the budget process has been improved considerably by changes in the budget document itself.

BUDGET MESSAGE IMPROVEMENT. A comparison of budget messages of recent years with that of 1947 shows that the message now places much greater emphasis on the relation of federal finances to conditions in the national economy. Graphs have been introduced to explain this relationship. At the same time, the budget message has been considerably shortened.

A MORE COMPACT BUDGET VOLUME. The budget for the fiscal year 1963 (presented in January 1962) was a major improvement over previous budget documents, which were in large-page size, about the thickness of a large-city telephone directory and filled with thousands of detailed schedules. The 1963 budget, in 300-odd pages of ordinary book size, included the facts and figures most users of the budget normally need, while the details concerning appropriations proposals and programs used by the congressional committees were put in an appended volume.

THE BUDGET IN BRIEF. Beginning in January 1950 the Bureau of the Budget has published each year a pamphlet presenting in popular form some of the most significant data relating to the budget and federal finance.

SPECIAL ANALYSES. The budget document has been improved by the addition of several special analyses. Since 1942 the budget has included an analysis of the cash budget and its relationship to the administrative budget. The 1963 budget presented for the first time an analysis of federal receipts and expenditures on a national income accounts basis. Since January 1950 the budget has contained an analysis of "investment, operating, and other expenditures," which divides budget expenditures into those that represent additions to federal assets, expenditures for nonfederal physical assets and other developmental purposes, current expenses for aids and special services, and other current operating expenses. Other special analyses have dealt with federal aid to state and local governments, federal credit programs, federal research and development programs, and federal government statistical programs.

OTHER CHANGES IN THE BUDGET DOCUMENT. The budget has been markedly improved by other changes also. "New obligational authority" recommended in the budget was first totaled and given separate treatment as recently as fifteen years ago. Obligations incurred were given separate treatment in the January 1958 budget, but were not summarized in a table by agency until the January 1962 budget. The comparison of obligational authority carried over, new obligational authority, and expenditures were summarized beginning with the January 1954 budget. In 1950 the budgets of all agencies were first broken down by program or activity, which made congressional appraisal easier, and in the same year a narrative statement for each appropriation or fund to indicate the results expected from expenditure of the funds requested was introduced. In the January 1962 budget a recapitulation of employment for the whole government was introduced into the budget document.

Improvements in Executive Phase of Budgeting

THE "TROIKA REPORTS." Beginning with President Kennedy's term of office and continuing in the Johnson administration, those agencies concerned with the overall budget and its impact on the economy—the Budget Bureau, the Treasury, and the Council of Economic Advisers—have submitted periodic reports to the President, reviewing the economic situation and recent budget trends and revising the budget totals when necessary. This informal group is now known as the "Troika," and it is regarded as having an important influence on budget and fiscal decision-making. The President ordinarily reads the Troika report very carefully and often initiates policy changes on the basis of information it contains. This coordination improves the budget process by keeping the Chief Executive continually informed of the economic situation and its implications for the budget, as well as of the impact of the budget on the economy.

PROGRAM BUDGETING. One of the most significant improvements in the Executive phase of the budget process is the trend toward program budgeting. By program is meant a group of activities that provides services directed toward the same policy objectives. In January 1947 only a few agencies, notably the Department of Agriculture, were providing in the budget a program and activity breakdown of their expenditures and new obligational authority.[12] Most budget estimates were broken down only into uniform object classifications (paper, travel, salaries, etc.). Beginning with the budget submitted in January 1950, a program breakdown of expenditures and appropriations by broad categories has been provided for most agencies.[13] In 1956 the classifications used for accounting, budgeting, and financial reporting were made consistent with one another.[14] A complementary development is the introduction of cost-type budgeting, where, through the use of accrual accounting, costs (goods and services consumed) are identified for each program. Currently about 70 percent of appropriations items are on this basis. The significance of program budgeting with accrual accounting is that it allows the Executive and Congress to evaluate the services provided by each of the federal government's programs in relation to their costs. More detailed breakdowns of program budgets are urgently needed to make them useful for analysis and evaluation of federal expenditures.

PROGRAM MEASUREMENT. Another complementary development is the emphasis, in recent budgets, on increased use of program measurements, and workload data. An attempt is made to identify and measure the services performed by agencies and programs, and to measure productivity. The usefulness of this is obvious—it provides a more precise basis for evaluating agency performance and comparing one program with another.

LONG-RANGE BUDGETING. There has been some development, in the Bureau of the Budget and the Executive agencies, of multi-year budgeting. Some agencies now plan programs and expenditures for several years ahead, and these are reviewed by the Bureau of the Budget. In view of the long-term nature of many projects and the

[12] U.S. Bureau of the Budget, *Improvements in Budget Presentation, 1947 to 1962*, Staff Paper (August 1962), p. 12.

[13] *Ibid.*

[14] *Ibid.*

increased concern in Congress and the Executive Branch with the implications for future spending of current program decisions, more emphasis on multi-year budgeting can be expected.

ORAL TESTIMONY ON THE OVERALL BUDGET. In addition to the improvements in Executive budgeting, the presentation of the budget to Congress has been improved in recent years through oral testimony by the Director of the Budget and the Secretary of the Treasury before one of the appropriations committees of Congress and the Joint Economic Committee. This enables the committee to gain some understanding of the total budget picture before it acts on the specific pieces assigned to the various subcommittees.

Efforts to Improve the Congressional Phase of Budgeting

The procedures used by Congress in carrying out its responsibilities to appropriate federal funds—to "control the purse strings"—have not changed basically for many decades, certainly not in the last thirty or forty years. Two efforts have been made to effect fundamental changes. The Legislative Reorganization Act of 1946 provided for a Joint Committee on the Legislative Budget, which was to meet early in each session of Congress, consider the President's budget proposal in light of economic conditions and efficiency, and set an annual ceiling on appropriations. The Committee died after it was unable to agree on a ceiling in 1947, and after its 1948 ceiling was not enforced.

A bill providing for the consolidation of all general appropriations into one bill for action by the House, the Senate, and the President was introduced in 1950. The procedure was tried in 1950, though the Omnibus Appropriation Act did not pass the Senate until August 4 and was not signed into law until September 6. Both because the delay was attributed to the new omnibus procedure (although it is not clear just how the appropriations process was delayed) and because it did not give the President the power to reject parts of the bill without rejecting the whole, it was abandoned in 1951.

Weaknesses in the Budget Process

The changes in the budget process, particularly on the Executive side, are notable, as the discussion above suggests. However, there are still weaknesses in the overall budget process that have been pointed out by various groups and individuals. Many of them deal with the legislative aspect of budget-making.

Coordination of Expenditure and Revenue Decisions by Congress

The budget is now taken up by Congress as a group of separate and unrelated parts. Taxes and expenditures are decided separately by separate committees in each house, and although the bills on taxes and appropriations are passed by vote of the whole House and whole Senate, there is little evidence that the two groups of bills are related closely to each other when they are considered.

Some way should be found to insure that Congress considers the total budget and the relation of expenditures and revenues to each other. As was indicated above, the Legislative Reorganization Act of 1946 sought to accomplish this with a Joint Budget Committee of Congress which would recommend a firm limit on total expenditures in a concurrent resolution after due consideration of revenues and the economic outlook, and before the various appropriations subcommittees began work on individual appropriations measures. For various reasons, the Joint Budget Committee did not work out satisfactorily; it was too large, and an overall expenditures limit was difficult to implement.

The Committee for Economic Development has recommended a Joint Budget Policy Conference.[15] This group, to include members of the congressional leadership, majority and minority representatives from the revenue and appropriations committees of both houses, and the Joint Economic Committee, would study the budget as a whole and issue a report, with the aim of providing communication among the revenue and appropriations committees of the two houses and the Joint Economic Committee.

Whatever is the best organizational solution, this weakness in the present budget process seems obvious, and some corrective action needs to be be taken.

Coordination of Appropriations Decisions

Under present procedure, appropriations are determined in both the House and the Senate in some thirteen separate appropriations bills, with little consideration in each case of the effect on total

---

[15] Committee for Economic Development, *Control of Federal Government Expenditure* (New York, 1955), pp. 15-16.

new obligational authority, total obligations to be incurred, or the likely level of total expenditures. The benefits and costs of the programs involved in each of the thirteen bills are not considered in relation to the benefits and costs of programs involved in other bills. Thus the individual Congressman is not encouraged to do what he should do—look at appropriations and expenditures as a whole and compare alternative programs in order to decide what changes in programs should be made in view of their costs and benefits. This in part reflects the fact that the appropriations subcommittees dominate appropriations decisions in both houses of Congress; seldom does either of the full committees make decisions as a unit.

This problem might be solved if meetings were held of the chairmen of the various appropriations subcommittees of the two houses, and if the two houses considered appropriations bills at more nearly the same time, as the Committee for Economic Development suggested.[16] The appropriations committees of Congress might be further encouraged to consider total appropriations if the President were given the power of *item veto*—to veto parts of appropriations bills that have passed both houses of Congress without vetoing the whole bill, as the CED also suggested.[17] Whatever particular institutional changes are made, some means must be found to encourage Congress to look at the total appropriation as well as the portions of it represented by the thirteen or so appropriations bills.

Flexibility in Changing Expenditures and Taxes

A number of groups and individuals have argued that the President should be given more power to change, at least temporarily, total federal spending and/or tax rates. The argument usually stems from a desire to make such actions more useful in evening out the ups and downs of the economy and the accompanying problems of unemployment and inflation. Under present arrangements it usually takes a very long time for Congress to approve a change in tax rates or spending authority.[18] Thus timely action to halt a recession or check an inflation may be precluded by the long time lag between a decision to do something and getting Congress to do it.

[16] *Ibid.*, pp. 17-18.

[17] *Ibid.*, p. 18.

[18] The 1963 tax cut took approximately one year and three months from its proposal by President Kennedy to clear Congress and become law.

Beginning with the January 1962 *Economic Report,* President Kennedy and President Johnson have proposed that the President be given standby authority to make temporary reductions in individual income tax rates and to accelerate expenditures. Congress has never acted on these proposals.

Several proposals to allow the Executive more flexibility in influencing tax rates and spending have been put forth in the last two or three decades. They have met with little success. The Congress is very reluctant to delegate its control over taxes and spending, even for temporary changes, to the President. Efforts will undoubtedly continue to be made to resolve this impasse, for many observers agree it would be a major improvement in using the budget as an economic tool.

CHAPTER IV

The Record: Federal
Spending and Taxes

A DISCUSSION OF federal budget policy can benefit from the perspective provided by the brief look, which this chapter takes, at the record of federal spending and taxation over the last 175 years, in particular in the period since 1930. This chapter will also consider the record of budget deficits and surpluses over the same period and finally will compare actual budget expenditures and receipts with budget estimates and discuss the reasons why they differ.

Trends in Federal Expenditures

Americans are somewhat inured to the colossal and the spectacular, but the growth of federal government expenditures over the last century and a half is still impressive when the statistics are shown. In 1794 the federal government spent about $7 million on a cash budget basis. In fiscal 1964 federal expenditures on a cash basis were over $115 billion, or more than 15,000 times the expenditures of 1794.

The pattern of this striking growth in federal expenditures is

FIGURE IV. Federal Cash Expenditures, 1794–1964[a]

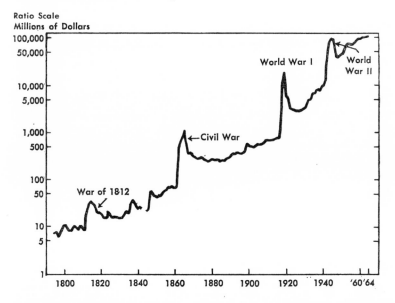

Sources: Data for 1794–1947 are from M. Slade Kendrick, *A Century and a Half of Federal Expenditure*, Occasional Paper 48 (National Bureau of Economic Research, 1955), Table B-1, pp. 74–77; and for 1948–64, from the U. S. Bureau of the Budget, *Budget of the United States Government* for fiscal years, 1961, 1963, 1965, and 1966; the 1843 data cover the period January–June 1843 only.

[a] Calendar years through 1842; fiscal years thereafter.

shown in Figure IV.[1] The most striking feature that emerges from the chart is the influence of war on the growth of federal expenditures. Large expansions of federal spending occurred during the War of 1812, the Civil War, World War I, and World War II. The trend of federal expenditures over the period of 175-odd years may be described as a series of plateaus. Wars have pushed federal spending sharply upward. With the return of peace, expenditures have fallen, but never to prewar levels because the wars left a heritage of interest and veterans' expenses. Between wars, expenditures showed long periods of relative stability, or even decline. But when another war came along, they were forced up, eventually leveling off at a higher plateau.

This growth of federal expenditures can be placed in a better perspective by comparison with the growth in other economic mag-

[1] Cash budget expenditure figures are used because they are more comprehensive than the administrative budget figures. (See Chapter II.)

nitudes over time. Over the 175-odd year period, the general price level has approximately tripled, or, to put it another way, the "value of the dollar" is perhaps one-third what it was in 1790. If we allow for changes in the general price level by expressing federal government expenditures in 1926 prices, the rise in spending looks much less formidable, as Figure V shows. Whereas expenditures expressed in current prices grew 15,000 times over in the 175-odd years, expenditures expressed in 1926 prices expanded about 6,300 times. Further, if allowance is also made for the fact that the population grew over forty-fold during the period, by expressing expenditures (in 1926 prices) on a per capita basis, it can be seen that federal expenditures per person (in 1926 prices) grew some 156 times over.

FIGURE V. Total and Per Capita Federal Cash Expenditures in 1926 Prices, 1794–1964[a]

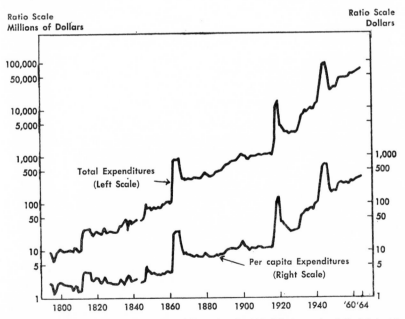

Sources: Expenditures in 1926 prices for 1794–1952 are from Kendrick, *A Century and a Half of Federal Expenditures*, pp. 79–82. For 1953–64 they were computed from data used for Figure IV and wholesale price index data taken from the *Federal Reserve Bulletin* and the *Economic Report of the President*. Per capita expenditures in 1926 prices for 1794–1952 are from Kendrick, *op. cit.*, pp. 84–87. For 1953–64 they were computed by dividing expenditures in 1926 by population taken from various issues of *Statistical Abstract of the U. S.*
[a] Calendar years through 1842; fiscal years thereafter.

FIGURE VI. Federal Cash Expenditures As a Percentage of Gross National Product, 1869–1964[a]

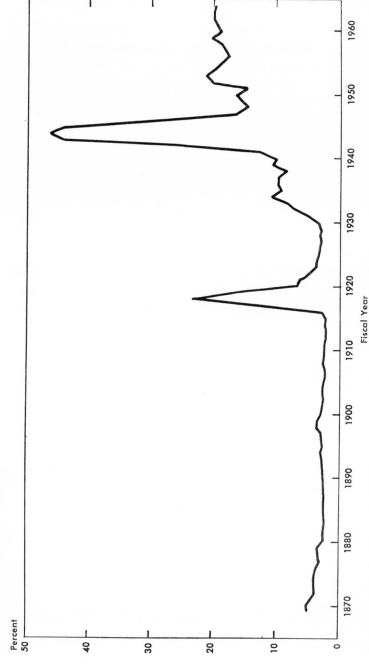

Percent

Fiscal Year

Sources: Data for 1869–1947 are from Kendrick, A Century and a Half of Federal Expenditures, pp. 10–11; and for 1948–64 from the Bureau of the Budget.
[a] Data are for fiscal years.

Perhaps the most significant measure of the growth of federal spending is the ratio of total federal spending to national output, or Gross National Product. Many types of federal spending can be expected to increase as the nation's economy expands—more output can mean that more highways have to be built, growth in urban areas requires more post offices, etc. Other types of spending—such as that for national defense—are related primarily to other influences, such as the international situation.

In any case, comparing federal expenditures with GNP is one way of measuring the importance of the federal government in the total economy. Of total federal spending, only "government purchases of goods and services" indicate the actual amount of resources of the economy that are absorbed by the federal government. The other components—transfer payments, net interest, subsidies, and grants to states and localities—represent income channeled through the federal government but given to the private sector or to the states and their subdivisions to spend. But such expenditures can be included in federal expenditures for comparison with GNP; they are part of the measure of total federal activity in the economy.

Figure VI shows that there has been a rise in federal expenditures relative to GNP over the period 1869-1964. From 5 percent in 1869, and a low of 2 percent in 1912-13, the percentage has risen to around 20 in recent years. As the chart makes clear, most of the rise has taken place since 1930. Except for the World War I years, federal expenditures remained about the same relative to GNP from 1869 to 1930. There was a rise in the percentage during the 1930's and a very sharp rise during World War II. It fell back somewhat after World War II but has remained high ever since. Purchases of goods and services, which measure the absorption of resources by the federal government, have increased at a slower pace because of the growth in importance of the federal trust funds.

Some light can be shed on the causes of the rise in this percentage since 1930 by classifying federal expenditures into "war-connected" and "other" and seeing how these have behaved relative to GNP. "War-connected" expenditures are military expenditures (including military grants to other countries), veterans' expenditures, and interest on the federal debt. The latter is included because the bulk of presently outstanding debt was issued in connection with war finance; the other two are quite obviously "war-connected." "War-connected" federal expenditures and "other" expenditures in relation to GNP since 1929 are shown in Figure VII. The chart indicates that although the rise in federal expenditures relative to GNP since 1930 is in considerable measure a reflection of the rise in "war-connected" expenditures, there was also a noticeable rise in "other" expenditures in relation to GNP, from less than 1 percent in 1929 to over 8 percent in 1964.

"War-connected" expenditures rose sharply relative to GNP during World War II, and then fell back drastically after the war as the country engaged in rapid demobilization. They rose again in 1950 with the advent of the Korean War and later the "Cold War" and have remained at about 12-13 percent of GNP since that time.

"Other" federal expenditures rose sharply relative to GNP during the 1930's, first under the impact of various federal relief and recovery programs designed to combat the very deep depression into which the country was plunged after 1930, and later as welfare programs such as old age and survivors' insurance and unemployment compensation were instituted. During World War II, and for most of the first ten years afterward, "other" expenditures by the federal government did not increase in relation to GNP. Since 1954, however, "other" federal expenditures have risen faster than GNP, and in 1964 they reached the all-time high of 8.3 percent of GNP.

Thus, the striking change during the period since 1930 reflects both an increase in war-connected and other expenditures relative to GNP and an increase in expenditures other than war-connected expenditures relative to GNP. That federal war-connected expenditures would cause total federal expenditures to rise relative to GNP was to be expected, given World War II, the Korean War, and the Cold War atmosphere. But the basis for the increase in "other" federal outlays since World War II may not be so obvious.

What has caused the increase in "other" expenditures relative to GNP during the last thirty years? Initially it reflected a host of depression-induced relief and welfare measures, as was mentioned above.[2] The relief and public works measures came to an end as

[2] Kendrick (*op. cit.*, pp. 32-33) estimates that 36 percent of total federal expenditures for the period 1930-41 were for programs begun after 1930 in response to the depression (relief, public works, aid to agriculture, social security, and unemployment benefits), and in 1935 this proportion was as high as 57 percent.

FIGURE VII. Federal "War-Connected" and "Other" Cash Expenditures As a Percentage of Gross National Product, 1929-64[a]

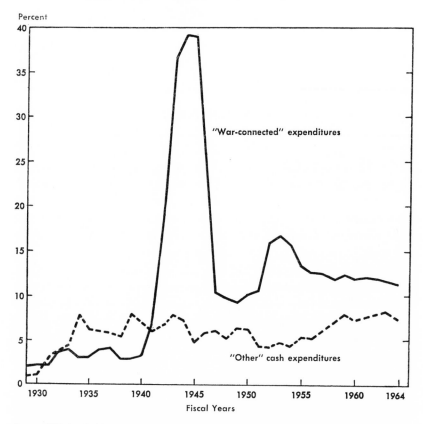

Percent

"War-connected" expenditures

"Other" cash expenditures

Fiscal Years

Sources: GNP data for 1929-38 are from Kendrick, *A Century and a Half of Federal Expenditures*, pp. 77-79; and for 1939-64 from the Bureau of the Budget.
[a] Data are for fiscal years.

recovery from the depression proceeded and preparation for World War II began in the late 1930's and early 1940's. Expenditures for agriculture and unemployment benefits fell as the economy moved toward high employment during World War II.

Since World War II, and more particularly since 1954, "other" federal expenditures have risen in large part because of the expansion of programs begun in the 1930's and because of changed economic conditions which would have raised expenditures under the existing programs in any case. Figure VIII shows the distribution of "other" expenditures for the fiscal years 1948-64, by dollar amounts and in percentages. It shows that the sharpest dollar increase in

FIGURE VIII. "Other" Federal Cash Expenditures, 1948–64

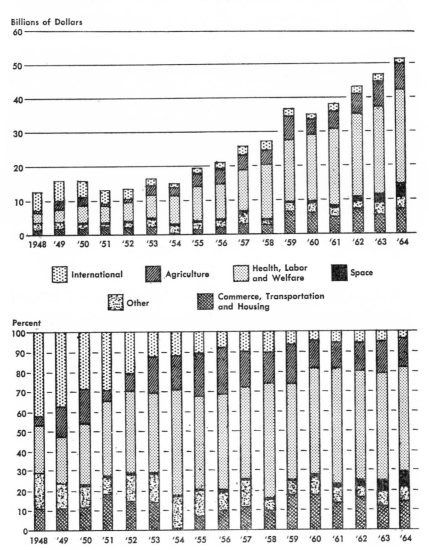

Source: Bureau of the Budget.

"other" expenditures over the postwar period has been in the Health, Labor, and Welfare category. Cash expenditures on these functions rose from $3 billion in 1948 to $27.3 billion in 1964. This reflected mainly increases in Old Age and Survivors Insurance payments and unemployment compensation benefits, which accounted for about 80 percent of the increase in this category. Other significant increases have occurred in expenditures for Agriculture, mainly for price support programs, and Commerce and Housing.

In summary, the striking feature of the record of federal expenditures is that they have risen relative to GNP since 1930, partly because "war-connected" expenditures have been forced up by the pressure of necessity, but also because of an apparent tendency since 1930 for "other" expenditures to remain higher relative to GNP than previously.

Trends in Federal Receipts

Three trends stand out when federal receipts over the last 175-odd years are studied. First, there has been a massive growth in receipts paralleling the growth in expenditures. Second, among sources of revenue, customs receipts (taxes on imported goods) were of overwhelming importance until the Civil War, but since then they have dwindled until now they are of very minor significance as a revenue source. That is, there has been a marked shift from "external" to "internal" revenue. Third, individual and corporate income taxes have become dominant among sources of revenue.

These trends are portrayed in Table 6. Although total receipts did not grow exactly in line with expenditures, as the government ran surpluses in some years and deficits in others, the general order of increase was the same. Customs duties provided about 90 percent of federal receipts in 1792, 1830, and 1860, but the proportion fell thereafter, until in 1964 customs duties accounted for about 1 percent of total federal receipts. The table shows the remarkable rise of individual and corporate income tax receipts; until 1910 there was no such tax (except during the Civil War), but by 1964 it accounted for 62 percent of total federal receipts from the public.

Table 6 also shows that employment taxes, those imposed on payrolls to finance social security, have risen sharply in importance

TABLE 6. Federal Receipts from the Public, Selected Years, 1792–1964[a]

Year	Individual income taxes	Corporation income taxes	Excise taxes	Employment taxes	Estate and gift taxes	Customs	Unemployment insurance deposits	Veterans' insurance premiums	Other	Total
In Millions of Dollars										
1792	—	—	—	—	—	3.4	—	—	0.2	3.7
1830	—	—	—	—	—	21.9	—	—	2.9	24.8
1860	—	—	—	—	—	53.2	—	—	2.9	56.1
1910	—	21.0	269.0	—	—	333.6	—	—	51.9	675.5
1930	1,146.8	1,263.4	565.1	—	64.8	587.0	—	—	550.8	4,177.9
1964	48,697.0	23,493.0	10,211.0	16,832.0	2,394.0	1,252.0	3,042.0	494.0	5,596.0	115,530.0
As a Percentage of Total										
1792	—	—	—	—	—	94	—	—	6	100
1830	—	—	—	—	—	88	—	—	12	100
1860	—	—	—	—	—	95	—	—	5	100
1910	—	3	40	—	—	49	—	—	8	100
1930	27	30	14	—	2	14	—	—	13	100
1964	42	20	12	15	2	1	3	—	5	100

Sources: Data for 1792–1930 are from Historical Statistics of the United States, Annual Report of the Secretary of the Treasury on the State of the Finances; and for later years from the Bureau of the Budget.

[a] Data for 1792 and 1830 are for the calendar year. All other figures are for fiscal years. Figures may not add to totals due to rounding.

since they were first introduced in the 1930's. They accounted for some 15 percent of federal revenue in 1964. Another relatively new feature of the federal tax system, estate and gift taxes, has made a minor contribution to the increase in revenue from internal taxes. Finally, although their *relative* importance did not increase, the *absolute* growth of receipts from federal excise taxes since 1930 has been significant; many of these taxes were introduced during World War II and remained in effect until 1965.

Thus the federal revenue system has undergone substantial change as the expenditures of the federal government have increased. Since World War I the tax system has been revolutionized through the adoption of, and increases in the importance of, income taxation. Reliance on income taxes has improved the productivity of the national revenue system, and in general it has been judged a fair method of raising revenues. While there are a number of difficult problems involved in federal taxation, our revenue system has, on the whole, served the nation well. As compared with the tax structures of most other countries, the tax structure of the U.S. ranks high in fairness as well as in productivity and compliance.

Cash Deficits and Surpluses

Since 1792 the federal government has run cash deficits in 72 years and surpluses in 101 years. The pattern of deficits and surpluses over the 175-odd year period is shown in Figure IX. The chart clearly shows that the large deficits have, for the most part, been incurred in wartime periods. There have been a large number of nonwar deficits, notably those of the 1930's, but the very large ones have mostly been war-induced.

Figure IX also shows that deficits are not peculiar to the period since the 1930's, as is sometimes suggested. In the period 1792-1920, there were forty-six deficit years and eighty-two surplus years, or a deficit in roughly one out of three years. The ratio is much higher, of course, for the more recent period; since 1930 there have been nine years of surplus and twenty-six years of deficits. Since World War II, however, there have been eight surplus years out of seventeen, which is about the same as the average since 1792.

Since 1792 the deficits have been cumulatively greater than the

FIGURE IX. Federal Cash Deficits or Surpluses, 1792–1964

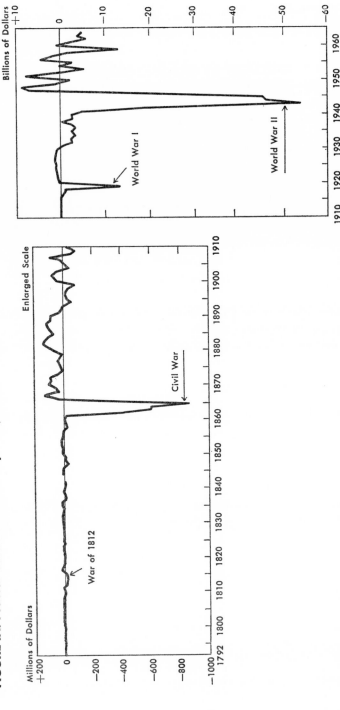

Sources: Expenditure data for 1792–1964 are from the sources given for Figure IV. Receipts data for 1792–1929 are from U. S. Department of Commerce, *Historical Statistics of the U. S.*, Series Y254. Figures for 1930–64 are from the Bureau of the Budget.

surpluses, and thus the federal government has accumulated a sizable public debt. In June 1964 the total federal debt was $312.5 billion.

Comparison of Estimated and Actual Receipts and Expenditures

Observers in the news media and politicians often comment on the disparity between budget estimates of expenditures or receipts (or the deficit or surplus) and the actual results. The implication is that the estimates of expenditures or receipts in the budget are not to be trusted, or are even twisted for political purposes.

A look at the record might incline one to believe that budget estimates *are* unreliable. Table 7 shows estimated and actual receipts and expenditures, and the differences between them. For the period 1947-64 the average annual error in expenditure estimates was some 6 percent of actual expenditures, and the average annual error in estimating receipts was almost 9 percent of actual receipts[3]

It should be remembered, however, that making estimates of receipts and expenditures involves forecasting international events and economic conditions for an eighteen-month period. The budget submitted in January is for the twelve-month period beginning the following July. In the six months from January to July, or at any time during the fiscal year, international upheavals or unexpected changes in economic conditions at home can drastically alter expenditure needs or the basis on which receipts are estimated. Further, when there is a change of administrations, the incoming President often requests Congress to change substantially the budget estimate of expenditures submitted by the outgoing President.[4] And

[3] At the same time it is interesting to note that if we take algebraic averages of the errors in receipts and expenditures estimates over the period—where the underestimates are canceled in part by overestimates—then the average excess of actual receipts over estimated receipts is about 1.4 percent of actual receipts, while the average shortfall of actual expenditures below estimated expenditures is 0.3 percent of actual expenditures.

[4] President Eisenhower reduced expenditure requests for fiscal 1954 some $7 billion below estimates in the Truman budget that was submitted for fiscal 1954. The large gap between actual expenditures for fiscal 1954 and the budget estimates is the result of the Eisenhower revision. For fiscal 1962 Eisenhower submitted a budget calling for $82.1 billion in expenditures. The incoming Kennedy Administration in the first four months in office requested a larger amount than

TABLE 7. Comparison of Federal Budget Estimates with Actual Receipts and Expenditures, 1947–64

(In billions of dollars)

Fiscal Year	Receipts				Expenditures			
	Estimate (1)	Actual (2)	(2)–(1) (3)	Error as percentage of actual receipts (4)	Estimate (5)	Actual (6)	(6)–(5) (7)	Error as percentage of actual expenditures (8)
1947	29,462	39,786	10,324	25.9	33,074	39,032	5,958	15.3
1948	36,894	41,375	4,481	10.8	36,692	32,955	− 3,737	− 11.6
1949	43,894	37,663	− 6,231	−16.5	39,086	39,474	388	1.0
1950	40,362	36,442	− 3,940	−10.8	41,235	39,544	− 1,691	− 4.3
1951	36,643	47,480	10,837	22.8	41,776	43,970	2,194	5.0
1952	54,299	61,287	6,988	11.4	70,775	65,303	− 5,452	− 8.3
1953	69,987	64,671	− 5,316	− 8.2	84,373	74,120	−10,253	−13.8
1954	67,827	64,420	− 3,407	− 5.3	77,749	67,537	−10,212	−15.1
1955	62,461	60,209	− 2,252	− 3.7	65,389	64,389	− 1,000	− 1.6
1956	59,685	67,850	8,165	12.0	62,093	66,224	4,131	6.2
1957	65,833	70,562	4,729	6.7	65,398	68,966	3,568	5.2
1958	73,053	68,550	− 4,503	− 6.6	71,240	71,369	129	0.2
1959	74,045	67,915	− 6,130	− 9.0	73,579	80,342	6,753	8.4
1960	77,100	77,763	663	0.9	77,030	76,539	− 491	− 0.6
1961	83,346	77,659	− 5,687	− 7.3	79,162	81,515	2,353	2.9
1962	81,700	81,409	− 391	− 0.4	80,232	87,787	7,555	8.6
1963	85,500	86,376	876	1.0	94,311	92,642	− 1,669	− 1.8
1964	88,400	89,459	1,059	1.2	98,405	97,684	− 721	− 0.7
Average of percentage differences............			8.9					6.1

Source: U. S. Bureau of the Budget. The following items were deducted from original budget receipts and expenditure estimates and actual figures: (1) Railroad Retirement Account, 1947–54; (2) refunds of receipts and capital transfers, 1947; and (3) interfund transactions, 1948–64.

finally, any budget estimate of expenditures and receipts is based on what the President asks the Congress to do. The persuasiveness and political power of the Executive obviously have a lot to do with whether his budget program will be enacted. And when the President's program is altered by Congress, this fact may be reflected in substantial differences between requested and actual receipts and expenditures.

---

was budgeted, and a large supplemental request was submitted in the summer of 1961 to support the defense buildup at the time of the Berlin crisis. As a result, actual expenditures in fiscal 1962 exceeded the Eisenhower request by some $7 billion.

CHAPTER V

Federal Budget Policy and Economic Policy

SINCE THE 1930's, it has been widely accepted that the federal budget can and should be used to level the ups and downs of the economy, that is, that federal budget policy should be an important part of stabilization policy. In the 1950's federal budget policy came to be judged not only as a stabilizing influence on the economy but also as a stimulant to economic growth. These ideas have been refined and expanded, and now it might be said that the most important criterion for judging federal spending and taxing plans is their combined impact on employment, prices, and economic growth. It is inevitable and right that those concerned with the federal budget, both in the Executive Branch and in Congress, should be concerned with its impact on the economy.

This chapter discusses the impact of budget policy on the nation's economy and how this must be considered in judging expenditure and tax policy.

Planned Spending

The federal budget makes its impact on the nation's economy largely through its effect on aggregate spending. Changes in the total of all spending by consumers, business, and government (federal, state, and local) affect output, employment, and prices. The federal government, through its tax and spending policies, can affect aggregate spending and therefore output, employment, and prices. In fact, this will happen whether the government plans it or not, so an understanding of the effect is important when budget and taxing plans are formulated.

First, the effect of spending on output, employment, and prices will be considered. The nation's output, or Gross National Product, is the sum of spending by consumers, business, and government on goods and services produced domestically (that is, excluding imports), plus foreigners' purchases of goods produced in this country.[1] Consumers spend on consumption goods, business spends on capital goods and inventories (investment), and government purchases goods from private industry and the services of its employees. For any period, total spending, including business spending on inventories, always equals output. That is, what is produced must by definition have been sold to government, consumers, businesses, and foreign countries, or else have gone into business inventories. But what makes the output level for any period what it is? What causes it to change?

Suppose at some selected output level the planned or desired spending of consumers, business, and government are added up, including planned additions to, or decreases in, inventories. Suppose also that what these sectors want to buy or add to inventories just equals the output it was assumed is produced. Under these circumstances employment and output will continue at the desired level. What happens if consumers, government, or business decide to spend more than before? Now total desired spending (including desired inventory accumulation) is greater than output. Businesses will experi-

[1] More precisely, Gross National Product is the sum of the value of all currently produced final goods and services in the economy for some particular period whether they are sold at home or abroad. In short, an estimate is made of how much of each "final" good or service is produced in a given period. This amount is multiplied by the market price of that good to get the value, and the two are added to get the total value of current goods and services produced. By "final" goods or services we mean goods or services that do not enter into the production of other goods; the production of "intermediate" goods, that is, goods used in the production of other goods or services, is excluded in arriving at a measure of the final product of the nation.

ence an unplanned reduction in their inventories, and to rebuild them they will seek to increase production, at least where this is possible. Conversely, a decline in the planned or desired spending by consumers, business, or government will produce an unplanned increase in business inventories, leading to a reduction in output.

The crucial force determining level of output, then, is planned spending by consumers, business, and government.

Planned total spending therefore is the crucial force determining the level of employment and hence of unemployment.[2] For employment of labor services tends to vary in the same direction as GNP. More output requires more hours of labor, and vice versa.

The relation of planned spending to prices and growth involves yet another concept: *potential* or *full employment* GNP. At any given time there is a maximum *potential* GNP that is consistent with full employment of the nation's labor supply. That is, given the size of the labor force, the average work-week and work-year, and the average productivity of labor per man-hour, there is some GNP that *could* be produced if the labor force were all employed, except for the usual frictional unemployment.[3]

Full employment GNP obviously does not remain unchanged

---

[2] Not all unemployment should cause concern. There is always an irreducible minimum of *frictional unemployment,* reflecting the fact that the economy is not perfect. It represents "normal" unemployment due to job switching and to the fact that all vacant jobs and all available workers are not in the same place at the same time, etc. The term "unemployment" will, therefore, be used here to mean unemployment in excess of normal, frictional unemployment. For more detail on the definition and measurement of frictional unemployment, see U.S. Congress, Joint Economic Committee, "The Extent and Nature of Frictional Unemployment," *Study of Employment, Growth, and Price Levels,* Study Paper No. 6 (November 1959).

How much unemployment can be considered to be merely frictional? There are differences of opinion on this question. Some say that frictional unemployment is no more than 2 percent of the labor force, but others are willing to accept higher figures. The majority opinion currently seems to be that an unemployment rate of 2 to 3 percent of the labor force would represent frictional unemployment only. An unemployment rate of more than 3 percent, then, clearly raises the problem of unemployment that concerns us.

[3] Full employment GNP is derived by multiplying the available labor supply by average labor productivity. The available labor supply is the total labor supply, less frictional unemployment, in man-hours. Suppose, for example, that the available labor supply is 140 billion man-hours (70 million workers working 40 hours a week 50 weeks a year). Then, if average productivity per man-hour were $5, full employment GNP would be $700 billion.

with the passage of time. We can expect growth in the labor force to increase the available labor supply if it is great enough to more than offset reductions in the work-week and work-year. Likewise research and development and the addition of new capital equipment will raise labor productivity.

Actual GNP, which we have just seen is determined basically by the planned spending of consumers, business, and government, may equal full employment GNP, or be less than full employment GNP, or even bump against and exceed it. If planned spending is weak and actual GNP is clearly less than full employment GNP, unemployment can be expected, since employment will vary with output and output will be less than that required for full employment of the labor force.

If planned spending is greater than output at full employment, that is, if consumers, business, and government are trying to buy more output (at current prices) than can be produced, there will be what is called an "inflationary gap" between planned spending and full employment GNP, and prices will tend to rise. This is sometimes termed an "excess demand" inflation, indicating that at full employment or capacity output the money demand for goods and services is in excess of that required to purchase this output at current prices.

Theories concerning inflation are very complex, and the speed and duration of inflation will not be analyzed in detail here. The essential fact to note is that when planned spending exceeds full employment GNP, prices tend to rise.

The government can therefore attack unemployment or rising prices by causing planned spending to vary. If the economy is at a level below full employment GNP, the government should seek to bolster spending. If it is bumping against full employment GNP and prices are rising, government should seek to restrain planned spending. However, a policy affecting only planned spending may not be sufficient to achieve the elimination of unemployment (above frictional unemployment) *and* stable prices at the same time. As the economy moves toward full employment, there is an upward pressure on prices. Plants are pushed to capacity, overtime and third-shift work become necessary, inexperienced workers must be hired, and unit costs thus tend to rise. In addition, unions are likely to press for higher wages, and sellers having monopoly power may be more inclined to raise prices.

Unless devices are available to restrain directly the upward pressure on prices and wages as full employment is approached, society—in using only measures to affect planned spending—may have to choose between some inflation and full employment or no inflation and less than full employment. This is illustrated in Figure X. Suppose government seeks only to affect total planned spending; it has no wage-price policy designed to restrain price increases *not* due to too much planned spending. All feasible combinations of the rate of unemployment and the rate of price increase are shown on a "possibility curve" such as the one in Figure X. On this curve, with no wage-price policy, at point A the rate of price increase is zero, but the unemployment rate is 4 percent, which is higher than the

FIGURE X. Illustrative Relationship Between Unemployment and Prices

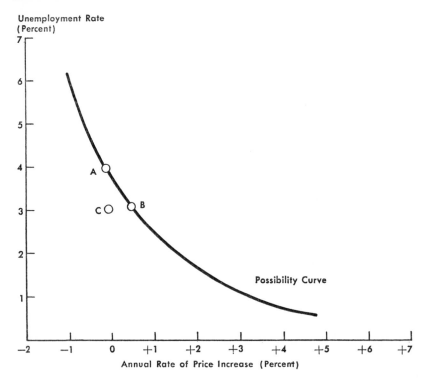

rate accounted for by frictional unemployment. When the unemployment rate is 3 percent, at B, which indicates that there is no unemployment in excess of what is usually considered frictional, prices rise by some 0.5 percent a year. Society can choose any point on the possibility curve by altering total planned spending. However, points like C, where unemployment is 3 percent and the rate of inflation is zero, can be attained only if some type of wage-price policy is possible which will restrain the upward tendency of prices and wages as total spending rises and pushes GNP toward the full employment level.

The shape and position of the possibility curve at any one time are thus determined by the structure of the economy and government wage-price policy. The curve might be changed through alterations in the basic characteristics of the economy, for example, by a weakening of union powers or a decrease in business monopoly power, or by stronger or weaker policies on the part of government to affect prices and wages. But at any point in time, policymakers have to choose. In the above example, those who are most worried about inflation might want point A. Those whose major worry is over unemployment might choose B. Opinions will differ as to which is desirable, and no one answer is "right" in any absolute sense.

Further, even if actual GNP and full employment GNP are equal at a particular time, without inflation, there is still the problem of growth. Suppose that the economy is at a point where actual GNP equals full employment GNP in some year, say 1966. As the labor force and labor productivity increase, full employment GNP increases. In 1967, then, full employment GNP might be (say) $50 billion more. If nothing occurs to increase private spending by $50 billion, or if the government takes no action, there will be a "gap" between planned spending and full employment GNP in 1967. In short, just achieving full employment GNP at stable prices "this year" is not enough; the economy is faced with the inexorable growth of full employment GNP, or potential output, which if not matched by increases in spending by government, business, and consumers, can lead to idle plant and equipment in industry and unemployment among the labor force.

The problem for policymakers, then, is to see that planned

spending by consumers, business, and government is such that the desired combination of employment and price level stability (of those combinations that are feasible) is achieved. This means that planned spending should be close to full employment GNP. If they "undershoot," and planned spending is deficient, there will be unemployment; if they "overshoot" and boost government and private spending above full employment GNP at current prices, prices will rise. And the problem is continuous—the steady growth of full employment GNP calls for continuous action to assure the growth of planned spending.

Full employment GNP is to some extent within the scope of public policy. Although public policy cannot do much about the rate of growth of the labor force, at least in the short run, the average work-week and work-year can be altered, at least under certain circumstances, such as a war emergency. There are also a number of ways to affect the growth in the productivity of labor, for example, through stimulating research and its application, education, etc.

But the immediate answers to the problems posed usually lie in influencing planned spending and *actual* GNP rather than potential GNP.

Federal Budget Policy and Planned Spending

The federal government[4] can exert considerable influence on spending and thus on prices, employment, and/or output by adjusting its expenditures or taxes—that is, by its use of fiscal policy.[5]

The Use of Fiscal Policy

The federal government affects planned spending by changing its own spending on goods and services and by causing consumer

[4] The responsibility for fiscal policy in the United States lies with the federal government. Although all levels of government—federal, state, and local—engage in making budgets and thus are engaged in budget policy, only the federal government is large enough for its budgetary decisions to have an extensive impact on the whole economy. In addition, it is difficult for a state or local government to pursue a policy designed to affect employment or prices, since other states or localities may pursue opposite policies and frustrate its efforts.

[5] Since interest in this chapter is in federal fiscal policy—how the federal budget affects the economy—the budget referred to is the *national income budget,* which (1) includes receipts and expenditures of the trust funds, such as OASI and the highway trust funds, (2) excludes purely credit transactions, and (3) treats tax receipts on an accrual basis and expenditures on a delivery basis.

and business spending on goods and services to change by affecting consumer and business income. First, what causes private spending to change?

Private (business and consumer) planned spending depends on several factors. One of these, which receives particular emphasis at the working level of public policy, is the relation of private spending to private disposable income, that is, disposable personal income plus disposable business income. Private disposable income is the income that is available for spending on goods and services by consumers and business firms, after taxes and other deductions. Consumer spending varies directly with disposable personal income, that is, the higher disposable personal income is, all other things being equal, the higher consumer spending will be, and vice versa. Likewise, the higher business income is, the higher investment by business can be expected to be, all other things being the same. In fact, businessmen often speak of the need for retained earnings for investment purposes.

But businesses and consumers save part of any increase in their incomes and do not spend it all. Also their spending does not fall by the same amount when their incomes fall. Thus private spending does rise when private disposable income rises (and vice versa) but not proportionately.

Private spending also is affected by other forces, in particular by the liquidity[6] of businesses and households, terms of lending or credit conditions, and expectations concerning future income and prices. When expectations change, when credit conditions or terms of lending change, or when the liquidity of businesses and consumers is affected, planned private spending for any level of private disposable income is affected. For example, if businesses' and/or consumers' expectations about the future suddenly become more optimistic, they will spend more at any level of private disposable income. If they become pessimistic, the planned spending of consumers and business at every level of private disposable income will be less. If firms and consumers become more liquid, say because of an increase in their cash holdings, private planned spending will increase for any level of private disposable income, and vice versa. Finally,

---

[6] Liquidity is measured by the relation to their incomes of cash, or assets readily convertible into cash, held by consumers and firms.

if credit gets tight and/or interest rates rise, private planned spending at any level of private disposable income can be expected to fall, and vice versa.

Suppose expectations, liquidity, and credit conditions are given. How can the federal government's budget action affect planned private spending? It can do so by changing the level of private disposable income. If the federal government *reduces* its tax "bite" out of the GNP, consumers and businesses will be left with larger *disposable* incomes. This will encourage more private spending, and GNP will rise. By contrast, if the federal government *increases* the tax bite out of GNP, this will reduce disposable income, reduce private spending, and cause GNP to fall. Alternatively, the federal government can affect private disposable income by changes in federal spending on goods and services. For when the federal government increases spending on goods and services, this results in added income for someone. The industries receiving orders for federal goods have more profits, and more wages are paid to the labor force in those industries. This increases business and consumer incomes and in turn affects business and consumer spending.

So the federal government can cause the level of private spending to change by affecting private disposable income—either by changing taxes or by changing federal spending, which eventually changes private incomes.

The effects of changes in federal spending, tax changes, and combinations of the two will be considered below.

Effects of Changes in Federal Spending or Taxes

EXPENDITURE CHANGES. Suppose the federal government increases its purchases of goods and services without changing tax rates. What will the effect of this be on the economy?

Other things being equal, increased expenditures by the federal government are expansionary. That is, they tend to raise output and employment (or, if the economy is already at full employment, to raise prices). Decreases in government purchases of goods and services, on the other hand, have an opposite, or restrictive, effect. In the discussion of how GNP is determined, it was pointed out that, given expectations, credit conditions, liquidity, tax rates, and government spending, GNP reflects planned spending. Clearly if government spending is increased, total planned spending and GNP will increase.

Suppose that GNP is at $500 billion and is equal to planned spending, so that there is no tendency for it to change. Assume also that consumers and business together spend 60 percent of any increase in private disposable income, that government taxes away 20 percent of any increase in GNP, and that the federal budget is balanced. Now suppose federal government purchases of goods and services are permanently increased by $10 billion. This might reflect purchases of more missiles or submarines, construction of new government buildings, or the hiring of more government employees. What will be the effect on GNP? The increase in total government spending of $10 billion will, in this example, cause output to rise by $19.2 billion, or almost twice the increase in government spending.

Why is this the case? Why does an increase in government spending cause a multiple increase in output? The answer is basically very simple. When the government spends another $10 billion (and keeps its spending at the new higher level), GNP or output will first rise by the amount of the increase in government spending, since the government is buying goods and services which represent output. However GNP rises *further* as the $10 billion of income generated in producing the output purchased by the government is received by consumers and business firms, because they use part of the income they receive to make expenditures on investment and consumption. Under the assumptions made, out of each dollar of income generated in producing the output purchased by the government, 20 cents will be taxed away, and of the 80 cents left, consumers and firms will spend 48 cents. So each dollar of income created will, by assumption, generate 48 cents of new private spending. GNP will rise by $10 billion due to the rise in government purchases; this will induce a rise in private spending of $4.8 billion, which in turn will generate new income and an additional $2.3 billion of private spending; and so on until the total change in GNP of $19.2 billion is achieved, as is shown in Figure XI. The total increase of $19.2 billion will be in the form of $10 billion more in government purchases of goods and services and $9.2 billion more private spending.

FIGURE XI. Illustrative Effect on GNP of a $10 Billion Increase in Federal Purchases

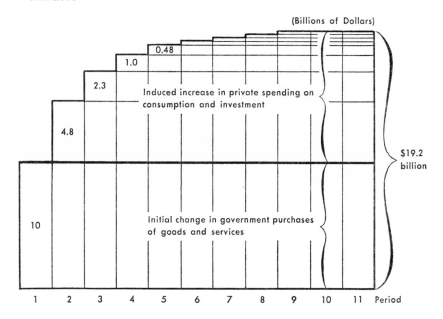

The whole process is reversed when there is a decrease in government purchases of goods and services. This will cause GNP to fall by 1.92 times the decrease in government purchases of goods and services.

One qualification needs to be made at this point. The net stimulative effects of a permanent increase in government spending may be reduced if it substitutes for private or state and local government expenditures that otherwise would have been undertaken. That is, if the government, for example, "sops up" investment opportunities open to the private sector, private investment outlays will be lower than they otherwise would be, and this will work against the stimulative effect. In the example given above it is assumed that this is not the case.

So increases in government spending on goods and services are generally expansionary, and decreases have a contracting effect. If there is slack in the economy, an increase in government expenditures on goods and services will cause output to rise. If the economy is already at full employment, an increase in government purchases of goods and services will perhaps bring about some increase in real output, but most certainly it will cause prices to rise.

CHANGES IN TAX RATES. Assuming that everything else (including government expenditures) remains the same, an *increase* in federal tax rates on incomes will increase tax revenues at any level of GNP, and vice versa. An increase in tax revenues means that private disposable income will be less, and this in turn means that, all other things being equal, private spending will be less. So whatever the level of GNP was previously, a tax increase will tend to reduce output (GNP) because it will reduce private spending. A tax cut, on the other hand, will tend to raise output by raising private spending.

For example, suppose the situation is the same as in the government spending increase case above. Suppose that, with GNP at $500 billion, the federal government decides to cut tax rates.[7] Specifically, assume that a cut in tax rates is planned so that, if GNP stayed at $500 billion, tax revenues would fall by $10 billion. This could be accomplished by cutting tax rates so that the percentage of the changes in GNP that is taken by taxes will fall from 20 to 18; if it is 18 percent instead of 20 percent, tax revenues at a GNP of $500 billion will be $10 billion less.

The effect of this $10 billion tax cut will be to cause the level of GNP to rise by $11.5 billion, or 1.15 times the tax cut of $10 billion. The process is similar to that in the case of the government expenditure increase. The cut in taxes will free $10 billion of income for the use of the private sector. Out of this increased income, the private sector will spend $6 billion more on consumption and investment. This will generate $6 billion of additional income, out of which will come about $1.08 billion in taxes.[8] The private sector will spend 60 percent of the remaining $4.92 billion, or $2.95 billion. This will generate another $2.95 billion of income, and the process will be repeated, until when it is worked out the total increase will be $11.5 billion.

Note that although a tax cut of $10 billion was assumed, actual tax revenues will not fall by this amount. A tax cut was planned

[7] The focus will be on changes in tax *rates,* since this is the more common way of changing taxes. Changes in exemptions also could be used. This works somewhat differently, but the general effects are the same.

[8] Note that the "tax bite" is now only 18 percent of the increase in GNP.

that will reduce tax receipts by $10 billion at the old level of GNP ($500 billion). But since the tax cut will have an expansionary effect and cause GNP to rise, the loss of revenue will be partially offset by the rise in GNP. The rise in GNP of $11.5 billion will generate 18 percent of $11.5 billion in tax receipts, or some $2.3 billion. The net effect on the budget deficit or surplus will be to decrease the surplus (increase the deficit) not by $10 billion, but by only $7.7 billion.

The same will be true in the case of the government expenditure increase mentioned earlier. Because it will promote a rise in GNP, an increase of $10 billion in government expenditures will not increase the deficit (or decrease the surplus) by the full $10 billion. The increase in GNP will bring in additional tax revenues of $3.84 billion (that is, 20 percent of the $19.2 billion increase in GNP), which will be a partial offset to the rise in government expenditures of $10 billion and will leave a deficit of $6.16 billion.

CHANGES IN EXPENDITURES AND TAXES. It has been noted that increases in government purchases of goods and services are expansionary and that decreases in tax rates are also. Obviously fiscal policy measures can involve combinations of tax and expenditure changes.

Assume that the economy is in a depression or a recession, or is growing slowly. (Actual output is less than full employment output, as is evidenced by unemployment in the labor force and idle capacity.) Then five combinations of tax and expenditure changes are possible:

1. The federal government can increase its purchases of goods and services, with no changes in tax rates.

2. The federal government can decrease tax rates without changing its purchases.

3. The federal government can simultaneously increase its expenditures on goods and services and lower tax rates, thus using both tools to raise GNP.

4. The federal government can increase both spending and taxes.

5. The federal government can lower spending and cut taxes, as long as the tax cut is sufficiently greater than the cut in government spending.

To illustrate some of these possibilities, the earlier original example, where GNP was $500 billion, will be used. Suppose that this is $50 billion short of full employment GNP, which is $550 billion. How large an increase in government spending will it take to raise GNP by $50 billion? Under the assumptions made about the percentage of changes in private disposable income spent and the percentage of additional GNP taken by taxes, for every dollar of increase in government spending, GNP tended to rise by $1.92. If GNP is to rise by $50 billion, then, under these conditions the required change in government spending alone is obtained by dividing $50 billion by 1.92. The result is $26 billion.

Achieving the desired increase in GNP by raising government spending alone would increase the deficit by $16 billion. The added $50 billion of GNP would produce $10 billion more of revenue (20 percent of $50 billion), which would partially offset the additional $26 billion of expenditures.

Now suppose that under the same conditions, the federal government attempts to raise GNP by $50 billion, using a cut in tax rates alone. The dollar tax cut, at the old GNP level, is obtained by dividing $50 billion by 1.15; thus $43.5 billion would be the needed tax cut. At the old GNP of $500 billion, this would mean a cut in tax rates which would lower the percentage of changes in GNP taken by taxes from 20 percent to 11.3 percent, or by 8.7 percentage points. The effect on the government's budget position in this case would be to produce a deficit of $37.6 billion; the $43.5 billion cut in taxes would be offset partially by a $5.7 billion rise in taxes (11.3 percent of $50 billion) due to an increase in GNP of $50 billion.

Thus to achieve the same increase in GNP, the tax cut required would be larger (in dollar terms) than the increase in government purchases of goods and services required. This follows from the earlier analysis of the effects of tax and expenditure changes; a change in government purchases would affect GNP more than would an equal dollar change in taxes, so a larger change in taxes would be required to achieve the same change in GNP. It should be noted also that because a larger tax cut would be required to achieve the same change in GNP, the tax cut would have a greater impact on the surplus or deficit of the government. The increase in government purchases would reduce the surplus or increase the deficit by $16 billion, whereas the tax cut achieving the same rise in

GNP would reduce the surplus or increase the deficit by $37.6 billion.

If the government desired, it could close the gap between actual and full employment GNP by increasing its purchases of goods and services, by decreasing taxes, or by combining both policies in various ways. For example, if it were decided to increase government purchases of goods and services by $10 billion, this alone would raise GNP by about $19.2 billion, and the tax cut needed to produce the remaining $30.8 billion increase in GNP could be calculated.[9] Similarly, any other possible increase in government purchases of goods and services, from zero to $21 billion, can be assumed, the increase in GNP it will likely effect can be calculated, and an estimate can be made of the change in taxes needed to make up the remainder of the desired $50 billion increase in GNP. The limits of these possible combinations of increases in government purchases and decreases in taxes are at one extreme, where government purchases alone are increased, and, at the other, where taxes alone are decreased. Thus the effect on the surplus or deficit, depending on the combination actually chosen, will be somewhere between $16 billion and $37.6 billion.

Finally, it should be clear that GNP can be increased by raising government purchases and taxes equally, that is, by "balanced" increases in government purchases and taxes. If a dollar change in government purchases affects GNP more than does a dollar change in taxes, then clearly an *increase* of $1 in government purchases will *increase* GNP more than a $1 *increase* in taxes will *lower* GNP. That is, increased spending by government raises GNP, and increased taxes lower GNP. But the expenditure change has more "punch" than the tax change, so on balance GNP will rise when government expenditures and taxes are raised equally. So equal increases in government spending and taxes can be planned, which will close the gap between actual GNP and the goal of full employment GNP. In short, balanced budget changes are not inconsistent with the use of expenditure and tax policy to maintain full employment and price stability.

As has already been indicated, equal increases in government purchases and taxes will pack a much lesser punch than will

---

[9] In this case it would be $26.2 billion.

changes in government purchases alone. So when actual GNP is below full employment GNP, smaller deficits will be incurred if full employment is achieved through expenditure increases than if it is attained through tax reductions.

The example given above dealt with a depression situation. The opposite case could just as well have been chosen, where planned spending at full employment GNP *exceeds* output (at current prices), that is, where there is an upward pressure on prices. The problem then will be to *reduce* planned spending. This can be done by lowering government purchases, or by raising taxes, or by lowering government purchases *and* raising taxes, or by lowering government purchases and *lowering* taxes. All the conclusions reached concerning the necessary changes in government purchases and taxes in each case and the effects on the budget will simply be reversed in this situation.

It should be recognized that the effects of tax and expenditure policy might not work out in actual practice exactly as has been described here. There may be changes in expectations or something else that would cause the relation of spending to income to vary and thus alter the final outcome. This discussion has assumed that "all other things are equal."

A QUALIFICATION: LIQUIDITY EFFECTS. Our discussion of the effects of changes in government expenditures or taxes must be qualified. Consider the case where GNP rises because government expenditures increase or taxes are cut. If the rise in GNP is not accompanied by an increase in money or other liquid assets, individuals and firms will have fewer liquid assets relative to their incomes. It is generally believed that individuals and firms will accept a poorer liquidity position only if interest rates or yields are higher. An individual will accept the greater risk of being caught with no cash, or assets readily convertible to cash, only if the return on his earning assets is higher. If these higher interest rates are required to induce the private sector to accept a poorer liquidity position, at least part of the expansive effect of increased government purchases or lower taxes will be offset by higher interest rates. As GNP rises, firms and individuals will try to obtain additional cash, or assets virtually as liquid as cash, by selling off their securities. This will drive yields up on securities generally until these individuals or firms are

satisfied with their poorer liquidity position. Private spending, particularly for residential construction and business investment in
plant and equipment, is to some degree sensitive to interest rates.
Higher interest rates *reduce* private investment to some extent, for
businessmen will forego projects when the cost of borrowing ap-
proaches or exceeds the return on the project. The higher interest
rates brought about by the efforts of firms and individuals to obtain
an acceptable liquidity position then will have some restraining
effect on private spending, thus offsetting, in part, the expansive
effect of the tax cut or expenditure increase. In short, the "multiplier effect" of tax or expenditure changes will be less because of
the liquidity and interest rate effects.

How much the impact of government fiscal actions is reduced
by interest rate effects depends on (1) the relation between interest
rates and the desired liquidity positions of firms and individuals and
(2) the relation between interest rate changes and changes in private
spending. This is a matter of some dispute, and no attempt to resolve it will be made here. In any case, this study is concerned with
the economic impact of *fiscal* actions—changes in government
spending or tax rates. The money supply and level of interest rates
are the prime concern and responsibility of the monetary authority
in the United States (the Federal Reserve System). The monetary
authority can do something about interest rates, so any effects of
this sort may be considered apart from fiscal action.

Restraints on Expenditure and Tax Changes

The economic impact of changes in federal spending or taxes has
been described, as well as how they can be used to combat situations
where there is unemployment and idle capacity or where excess
demand results in inflation. What "mix" of expenditure and tax
policy changes is appropriate? Some of the practical problems in
the use of expenditure or tax changes are indicated briefly in this
section.

In the case of both changes in government purchases of goods
and services and tax rate changes, there are lags that must be considered. There is the *recognition lag*—the time between the occur-
rence of an economic event (say the beginning of a recession) and

its observation and verification. Fiscal policymakers have various indicators at hand to check the health of the economy, such as the quarterly GNP estimates, the monthly price index for consumer and wholesale goods, monthly unemployment data, and a wide variety of "leading," "coincident," and "lagging" indicators issued by the Department of Commerce. Ideally it would be desirable to be able to predict future changes in output, prices, or unemployment that will require corrective action by the fiscal authorities, but in the present state of knowledge, usually they are trying to correct undesirable movements in output or prices that are already under way.

There is also a lag between the recognition of an economic condition which requires action and the action itself. This is termed the *administrative lag*. The speed with which policies may be changed involves political considerations as well as some technical ones. As between changes in net taxes and changes in government spending, the political aspects make the lag less for expenditures than for taxes, but the technical considerations work the other way. Although changes in both appropriations and tax rates, exemptions, and brackets must be legislated by Congress, the President can to a limited extent vary the rate of expenditure during a given period through apportionment of appropriations by the Bureau of the Budget, as was seen previously. On the other hand, a given legislated change in tax policy may be put into effect much faster than a given expenditure change. The effect of changing rates, brackets, or exemptions on private income is immediate, because taxes are withheld on individuals and are computed on an accrual basis by corporations. In the case of expenditure programs the effect is not felt as quickly. In the first place, it takes time to plan the projects on which public funds will be spent. Second, even if the plans are already at hand, public projects cannot be put into operation at a moment's notice. There are many legal and institutional details, such as contract-letting and materials procurement, which must be accomplished before work can actually be undertaken. And once it is started, a public works or other anti-recession program cannot be ended at will. Projects in progress have to be completed if they are to function or to avoid deterioration, even though the need for additional spending for stabilization purposes may no longer exist.

There is, finally, the *operational lag*. This is the time which elapses from the beginning of a policy change to the attainment of the desired results. On this count, tax changes are clearly more effective. When rates or exemptions are changed, the full effect occurs immediately and continues as long as the new policy is in effect.

In general, both tax and expenditure changes are slow and somewhat clumsy instruments of policy, largely because of the need to obtain legislation from Congress for all significant policy changes. A recent study has indicated that discretionary fiscal action has been of very limited importance in reducing the severity or duration of postwar recessions because of its modest use and problems of timing.[10]

Presidents Kennedy and Johnson have sought to improve the countercyclical powers of the government by asking Congress to give the President standby power to cut tax rates temporarily and to initiate public works programs to combat unemployment. Similar standby power to reduce taxes was proposed by the Commission on Money and Credit and the Committee for Economic Development. As was pointed out earlier, Congress has not granted any of these requests, apparently feeling that this would be an excessive delegation of its authority to the Executive.

The Lewis study notes several factors that have prevented better use of discretionary fiscal action.[11] One can be described as "prior commitments and long-range goals." For example, President Truman, having just been elected to office in a campaign featuring charges of Republican "fiscal irresponsibility" in the tax cut of 1948, was naturally reluctant to propose a tax cut in 1949 to combat that recession. Another factor has been the desire to maintain public and business confidence; policymakers have been reluctant to take a discretionary fiscal action because explicit recognition of the existence of a recession might have undesirable psychological effects. In recent recessions also the fear of an impending need for sharp increases in defense outlays has made Presidents reluctant to take policy action in the early stages of recessions for fear of inflationary effects during recovery periods. Public concern over deficits has also operated to limit the use of discretionary fiscal pol-

[10] Wilfred Lewis, Jr., *Federal Fiscal Policy in the Postwar Recessions* (Brookings Institution, 1962). See especially p. 22.
[11] *Ibid.*, pp. 20-23.

icy to combat a recession. And finally, emphasis on "efficiency" in the rate of expenditures has at times restrained action against recessions.

The timing problems and other restraints on the use of discretionary tax and expenditure changes by the federal government have not been as serious as they might have been because there are also automatic tax and expenditure changes (or their equivalent) built into the federal budget, and these work to cushion the economy against recession and to restrain it during boom periods. How these *automatic fiscal stabilizers* can be properly combined with discretionary policy, and the resulting implications for the federal budget, are discussed below.

The Fiscal Stabilizers

The fiscal stabilizers are automatic tax or expenditure changes built into the federal budget which work to cushion private disposable income against decreases in GNP and to restrain the growth of private income when GNP rises. By so doing, they moderate the fall of private spending when GNP falls, and limit the increase in private spending when GNP rises. Thus GNP falls and rises less than it might otherwise because of their stabilizing effect. They are automatic in the sense that they depend on the level of GNP and they become effective when GNP changes, without any decisions by the Executive or Congress being necessary.

The two major fiscal stabilizers of the federal government are (1) transfer payments, which are paid by the federal government to the aged, the poor, the unemployed, and other needy people in the nation, and (2) taxes.

Most transfer payments vary inversely with GNP; as GNP rises they fall, and as GNP falls, they rise. The principal transfer payment, unemployment compensation, rises when GNP *falls* (since unemployment increases), and vice versa.

If, for example, a change in private spending causes GNP to fall, the effect of unemployment compensation payments will be to moderate the fall of private disposable income. And, as has already been seen, if the fall of disposable income is checked, the fall in GNP will also be moderated.

The progressivity of the tax structure has the same effect. A tax system is *progressive* if the ratio of taxes to income increases as income increases. The personal income tax is progressive because of: (1) the personal exemption of a specified amount of income from taxation; and (2) the fact that marginal rates increase as individuals move to higher brackets. Even if every dollar of income were taxed at the same rate but individuals were allowed to exempt a given amount of income from taxation, the tax system would still be progressive. For GNP would have to reach a certain level before any taxes would be paid at all. This by itself would mean that the ratio of taxes to GNP would rise as GNP rises, and vice versa, which is the definition of a progressive tax system.

The tax system is progressive also because marginal tax rates rise as one moves up to higher brackets. This means that the percentage of changes in GNP taken by taxes increases as GNP increases—as more people move up into higher tax brackets.

The importance of these automatic stabilizers in maintaining disposable personal income when GNP falls can be clearly seen in Figure XII, which shows changes in GNP and disposable personal income by quarters for the period 1953-64. As can be seen, the fluctuations in disposable personal income were much less than those of GNP, and this reflects operation of the "automatic stabilizers."

The importance of the automatic stabilizers to the economy in the postwar period has been very great. Lewis found that "the built-in fiscal stabilizers have made a substantial contribution to the stability of the postwar economy."[12] Similarly, the Council of Economic Advisers, in its 1963 *Report,* noted that "automatic fiscal stabilizers have made a major contribution in limiting the length and severity of postwar recessions."[13]

However, the role of the automatic fiscal stabilizers should be clearly understood. They act to *stabilize* the economy, to prevent sharp upward and downward movements of GNP. They do not insure that the level of GNP around which the movements of GNP are moderated is full employment GNP. If the economy were at full employment, and something brought about a decrease in planned private spending, the automatic fiscal stabilizers would reduce the impact on GNP of the fall in spending, but they would not reverse

[12] *Op. cit.,* p. 15.
[13] *Annual Report of the Council of Economic Advisers* (1963), p. 67.

**FIGURE XII. Quarterly Changes in GNP and Disposable Income
1953–64ᵃ**

(Billions of Dollars)

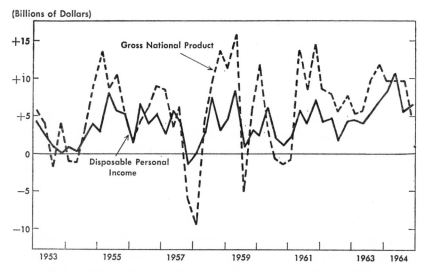

Sources: U. S. Department of Commerce, *Survey of Current Business* and *National Income and Output.*
ᵃ Seasonally adjusted annual rates.

it. Discretionary action would be required to restore full employment GNP unless something else happened to restore private spending.

The Deficit or Surplus
as a Measure of Fiscal Action

Popular discussion of the effect of the budget on the economy
—in the press, in Congress, and even to some extent among economists—often focuses on the current budget deficit or surplus. It
is said that when the federal government runs a deficit, the effect on
the economy is expansionary, and when it runs a surplus, the effect
is restrictive.[14] As a matter of fact, the actual federal government
surplus or deficit reveals nothing about the "tightness" or "loose-
ness" of the government's fiscal program, and use of this standard
often leads to wrong conclusions.

The reason government deficits or surpluses are a poor guide

[14] Reference here is to a surplus or deficit in the national income budget.

for interpreting fiscal policy is that they reflect not only the decisions of Congress with regard to spending and tax rates (discretionary fiscal action) but also the response of tax revenues and transfer payments to changes in GNP (the automatic stabilizers). Even with no change in tax rates or budgeted expenditures, the federal deficit or surplus varies as GNP varies. The federal deficit may increase because GNP falls (tax revenue falls, and transfer payments rise). Or the deficit may increase as a result of discretionary action—a tax cut or an increase in expenditures—when GNP is rising. The two deficits are not the same in terms of their economic impact: one occurs as a result of a fall in GNP (and moderates that fall), while the other helps produce an increase in GNP. The impact of fiscal policy in the two cases cannot be equated; the size of the federal deficit is not a reliable measure of fiscal policy.

These distinctions may be made clearer with the aid of a graph developed by the Council of Economic Advisers in its 1962 report.[15] The given budget or fiscal program (given tax rates and expenditures, except for transfer payments and others, which vary with GNP) is indicated by the budget line labeled A in Figure XIII. At any point on this line, the level of budgeted expenditures (those *not* varying with GNP) and tax rates are the same. The vertical axis shows the government's surplus or deficit (in the national accounts budget); the horizontal axis shows the level of GNP. Since transfer payments fall and tax revenues increase as GNP rises, the given fiscal program produces deficits at low levels of GNP, but the deficit is reduced and turns into a surplus as GNP rises. The automatic change in the federal government's deficit or surplus resulting from changes in GNP, with a given fiscal program, is shown by movements along budget line A.

An alternative fiscal program, with different tax rates or expenditures, is reflected in a shift in the budget line.[16] Suppose that the fiscal program is modified by a tax cut or expenditure increase, illustrated by line B. The deficit would be greater (the surplus less) at every level of GNP.

So the federal government's deficit or surplus in a particular period depends on two things: the fiscal program and the level of GNP. These two are not independent of one another, however. The

[15] See pp. 78-80.
[16] This is not always the case, as will be noted below.

FIGURE XIII. Effect of Level of Economic Activity on Federal Surplus or Deficit

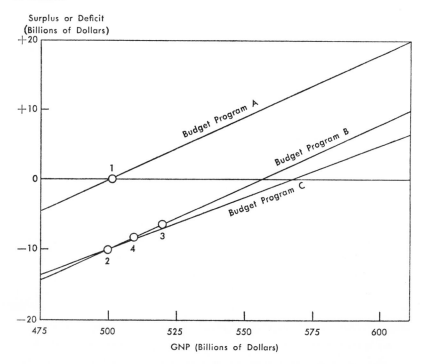

choice of a fiscal program will affect the level of GNP. If expenditures are increased and the budget line shifts downward, GNP will rise, as is illustrated by the example on page 63. This example started with a balanced budget (point 1 in Figure XIII). A $10 billion increase in expenditures would shift the budget line down by $10 billion to B, point 2. This would cause GNP to rise by almost $20 billion (point 3), making a net increase in the deficit of about $6 billion. A tax cut of $10 billion would shift the budget line down to C, point 2. The tax cut would produce a smaller increase in GNP (point 4) and a larger increase in the deficit than would an increase in expenditures.[17]

[17] Budget line C has a different slope than A or B because the percentage of changes in GNP taken by taxes is changed. That is, a reduction of this percentage by 2 points would increase the deficit by $10 billion at a GNP of $500 billion, but would increase it by $12 billion at a GNP of $600 billion. So the budget line is less steep than before.

One further point deserves attention. The budget line will not always shift when there is a change in the fiscal program. Suppose government purchases and taxes are increased equally for every level of GNP.[18] This will not affect the budget line because the effect of the increase in government purchases on the deficit is just canceled out at every level of GNP by the increase in taxes. But the fiscal program has changed; the equal rise in government purchases and taxes would, as we saw, affect the level of GNP. So the budget line is not an unambiguous indicator of a fiscal program. This is simply because it measures the impact of different fiscal programs by the surplus or deficit they produce at a given level of income. And as has been seen, the impact of fiscal policy is not measured by the surplus or deficit for some level of GNP. It is the level of government purchases and taxes that produces the deficit or surplus that matters. A surplus of $10 billion (at some level of GNP), with spending of $90 billion and tax revenues of $100 billion has a very different impact from a surplus of $10 billion resulting from expenditures of $190 billion and tax revenues of $200 billion.

In summary, the deficit or surplus that the federal government actually runs is no measure of the impact of fiscal policy because it reflects both the automatic responses of taxes and transfers to changes in GNP and discretionary changes in tax rates and spending. Second, the deficit or surplus at any level of GNP (whether achieved or not) is also not an adequate gauge of the fiscal program, at least if a fiscal program is considered to be one with a given impact on the economy, for it is the level of spending and taxes that produces the deficit or surplus that matters, not the deficit or surplus itself.

Although the deficit or surplus does not provide a guide to fiscal action, the proper use of fiscal policy involves certain implications for budget balance, that is, for the likelihood of continued deficits or surpluses. This is taken up in the next chapter.

Summary and Conclusions

This chapter has considered the general impact of federal spending and taxation within the framework of GNP determina-

---

[18] Which would be approximately the case if taxes are increased by changing exemption levels rather than marginal tax rates.

tion. Increases in government purchases of goods and services are expansionary, and increases in tax rates are restrictive; spending increases are more potent per dollar, in their impact on GNP, than are tax rate changes. Also there are quite lengthy time lags in the execution and effect of expenditure and tax rate changes, which make continuous adjustment difficult. However, the automatic fiscal stabilizers—the progressive personal income tax and transfer payments—smooth out fluctuations in GNP even though they cannot be entirely eliminated. Timely and appropriate use of discretionary tax and expenditure changes is therefore needed to at least moderate any tendency for prices to rise during periods of inflationary pressure, and to assist in restoring full employment when the economy is operating below its potential. The success of such action depends also on the structure of the economy and the wage-price policies followed.

CHAPTER VI

Fiscal Policy and the Budget Program

THE FEDERAL GOVERNMENT can work toward achieving some combination of a low rate of unemployment and price stability by varying either expenditures or tax rates, or both. By doing both in differing degrees, the federal government can achieve its goals and can do so with a balanced budget, a surplus, or a deficit. The question now arises: what is the best "mix" of expenditures and taxes? Does following this best mix lead to deficits, surpluses, or a balanced budget? What reliance should be placed on the "automatic fiscal stabilizers"?

A Suggested Budget Policy

When discretionary fiscal policy is used, one very important consideration must be taken into account in deciding on the proper mix of tax rate changes and changes in expenditures: that is that government expenditures and taxes play fundamentally different roles in the economy. When the government purchases goods or services, it is allocating resources between the public and private sectors, according to the preferences of its citizens. This being so, it would seem that the allocation function of government expenditures

80

should not be obscured by using them for fiscal policy reasons, that is, to affect the level of economic activity. Expenditures should ideally be set at that level which, assuming full employment, achieves the public's desired allocation of resources between the production of public goods and private goods. If the public wants one-fifth of full employment output to go to defense, then expenditures should be set to produce this result. Or if it would rather have (say) more automobiles and recreation, public expenditures should be adjusted accordingly.

Given the level of public expenditures that is preferred by society—in terms of the allocation of resources between the public and private sectors—tax rates and other transfers should generally be adjusted so as to produce full employment with price stability. The burden of adjusting total spending so that there is neither persistent unemployment nor inflation should fall mainly on taxes.

However, it should be recognized that tax rate changes are not a perfect weapon for combating economic fluctuations. They may disrupt business planning and result in a deterioration of the tax system. Furthermore, the current political situation is such that even though reliance on tax rate changes might be more desirable, they are difficult to achieve in the short run.[1] If discretionary fiscal policy is to be used in the present setting, changes in government spending must be used along with tax rate changes.

What are the implications of this for budget balance? Basically, it depends on private spending propensities. Once government expenditures are set, if private spending is high, then tax rates will have to be set high to avoid inflation. This will tend to produce budget surpluses. On the other hand, if private spending is weak, then tax rates may have to be adjusted downward to achieve full employment output; and with given government expenditures, this may mean that a deficit must be run to achieve full employment. It could also happen that a balanced budget, given the size of government expenditures, might be consistent with full employment output without inflation.

This leads to the conclusion that if discretionary fiscal policy is to be used to achieve the objectives assumed, then the budget sur-

---

[1] The Revenue Act of 1964 has demonstrated that tax reduction can be effective in promoting higher incomes and employment. But there still is no indication that the Congress is more receptive to the use of taxation for countercyclical purposes.

plus or deficit is not a direct object of public policy. Persistent deficits may be necessary to achieve full employment, or it may be possible to balance the budget or even run surpluses. If fiscal policy is used properly, the level of taxes and expenditures will be set to achieve full employment without inflation and to achieve the desired allocation of resources; then the surpluses or deficits will be allowed to occur where they may.

Although this general approach has the endorsement of the Johnson administration (and before it, the Kennedy administration), of important business and labor groups, and of expert bodies such as the Commission on Money and Credit, it does not seem to be understood by the general public. It seems "fiscally irresponsible" to show so little interest in a balanced budget. In particular the implication that prolonged periods of weak private demand must produce sizable and perhaps persistent federal deficits, and thus a growing national debt, produces strong opposition that cuts across partisan lines.

At this point another consideration should be noted. The federal government also can use monetary policy and debt management policy[2] in its effort to achieve high employment without inflation. Throughout this discussion, the liquidity of the private sector has been assumed as "given." However, monetary policy and debt management policy both affect the liquidity of the private sector. They are somewhat complex, and there is considerable controversy about their effectiveness, but to the extent that they are effective, they may be substituted for fiscal policy. For example, given a certain level of government expenditures, and assuming that private demand is weak, tax reductions and a deficit may not be necessary to reach full employment if monetary policy and debt management policy can produce the needed increase in private spending by increasing the liquidity of the private sector. Or a high propensity to spend on the part of business and consumers need not necessarily call for high tax rates and a surplus if the same result can be achieved

[2] Monetary policy calls for action to vary the quantity of money or, more generally, the quantity of "liquid assets" in the economy. Debt management refers to all steps taken by the federal government, including the Federal Reserve System, that affect the composition of the publicly held debt, particularly its maturity composition.

through monetary or debt policy by reducing the liquidity of the private sector.

The budget policy suggested here is one where tax rates are adjusted, given the size of government expenditures, to produce full employment without inflation, and where automatic fiscal stabilizers moderate the impact of short-run swings in business activity. This does not mean that tax rates will have to be continuously adjusted, however. In fact, they probably should not be varied at intervals of less than three to five years, given the technical problem of estimating the magnitude of the rate change needed and the difficult procedure of securing tax rate changes from Congress. At times, changes in government spending may have to be used in place of, or as a complement to, changes in tax rates. The important points are that: (1) discretionary fiscal policy should consist of tax rate changes as well as variations in expenditures; (2) tax rates should be set to achieve our economic objectives and not primarily in consideration of their effect on the deficit or surplus; and (3) continued emphasis should be laid on automatic fiscal stabilizers for their cushioning effect.

Alternative Budget Policies

The budget program discussed here is by no means universally accepted. Many citizens, as has been noted, object to planned deficits. Other observers have little faith in the ability of the President and his advisers, and ultimately of Congress, to select the proper magnitude and timing for tax rate changes. Still others worry about the effect of such a budget on the public's attitude toward "fiscal responsibility." This section will examine these objections briefly as well as some alternative budget proposals and their weaknesses.

The Annually Balanced Budget

Judging from a Gallup Poll taken in 1962,[3] public pronouncements by Congressmen, and "letters to the editor," a sizable segment of the public believes that the federal government should strive to

[3] See the *New York Times* of Aug. 2, 1962. Seventy-two percent of those polled were opposed to a tax cut if it meant that the federal government would go further into debt.

balance the budget every year, or in any case that the federal government should not plan to run deficits. Those who hold this view usually draw an analogy to the family or business budget. Since continuing deficits by individual families or businesses can mean economic ruin in the form of bankruptcy and loss of credit rating, it is argued that this is true also of the federal government. Still more general is the view that the goal of an annually balanced budget is essential fiscal discipline to control the built-in tendency of the federal government to overspend.

There is something to be said for the concern for "fiscal responsibility" expressed by those who favor an annually balanced budget. If private spending is persistently weak, and the government in raising expenditures or lowering taxes to maintain full employment has to run persistent deficits, the public may begin to feel that extending public services is essentially costless, and this may lead to an overextension of public services.[4] However, an analogy between private bankruptcy and public bankruptcy is fallacious, as will be seen in the next chapter.

If these arguments were taken seriously, the annually balanced budget could have extremely pernicious economic effects. Should the economy go into a slump, tax revenues would automatically decline, and the budget would begin to show a deficit. To offset this, the government would have to either decrease government spending or raise tax rates. In either case the effect would be to lower the level of GNP still further, which would intensify the recession. The attempt to maintain a balanced budget would also work to accentuate any rise in GNP, accelerating the danger of inflation. In short, a serious attempt to maintain an annually balanced budget would reinforce any existing movement toward recession or inflation.

Whatever the merits of the case for an annually balanced budget as a means of promoting fiscal responsibility, they are far outweighed by the perverse effect such a budget policy would have on the level of employment and prices. No responsible person could seriously advocate such a budget policy unless he could show that booms and slumps in business activity can be controlled effectively by other devices.

---

[4] On the other hand, if the federal government runs persistent surpluses, then the public may feel that public services are really more costly than they are, and this may lead to "underspending."

Automatic Stabilizing Budget Proposals

While a policy of annually balanced budgets would only accentuate the ups and downs of the economy and thus the problems of inflation and unemployment, a discretionary policy designed simply to promote full employment and stable prices also poses problems.

First, heavy reliance on the judgment of the Executive and Congress to choose the proper level of tax rates and government spending suffers from the inadequacy of present forecasting techniques. Judgment about required tax rates or expenditures involves a substantial amount of guesswork about future levels of output, prices, and employment, and the possibility of error is ever present. Another problem is that heavy reliance on discretionary policy can easily lead to primary emphasis on expenditure rather than tax changes, because the reaction against deficits caused by higher spending seems to be milder than that against deficits brought about by tax cuts. And finally, there is justifiable concern that such a policy of "letting the deficits or surpluses occur where they may" removes the restraint on government spending provided by the goal of an annually balanced budget, where every new expenditure has to be "paid for" by the clear and unequivocal act of raising the necessary tax revenues.

There is a group of proposed budget policies designed to avoid the problems of either the annually balanced budget or discretionary policy while preserving their virtues.

Perhaps the most widely known of these in this country is the Committee for Economic Development's "stabilizing budget" proposal.[5] The proposal has had significant impact on the thinking of many influential citizens because it emanates from an organization of highly respected, top-echelon businessmen from all areas of industry and commerce. Briefly the CED proposal centers around the idea of setting federal government purchases of goods and services at a "needs" level, fixing tax rates so that a "moderate surplus" would be generated at a "high employment" level of GNP,[6]

[5] See their publications *Taxes and the Budget: A Program for Prosperity in a Free Economy* (1947) and *Fiscal and Monetary Policy for High Employment* (1961).

[6] Both CED documents define "high employment" as a situation where 96 percent of the labor force is employed. The "moderate surplus" is set at about

and then letting the automatic fiscal stabilizers work to even out the periods of prosperity and recession in the economy.

The CED sees several virtues in the program. First, it would stabilize the economy; as has been noted above, the automatic fiscal stabilizers have been effective in the postwar period. Second, it would provide at least some of the budget discipline of the annually balanced budget; every new expenditure would require higher tax rates to keep the planned surplus at high employment the same.[7]

Finally, the CED envisages that the program would permit some retirement of the public debt, presuming that the economy would tend to fluctuate around the high employment level of GNP and that the surpluses run in good years would be cumulatively greater than the deficits in bad years.

Very similar proposals have been made by Milton Friedman[8] and Gunnar Myrdal.[9] The Friedman proposal differs mainly in making specific recommendations on monetary policy and in proposing that federal deficits and surpluses be financed by issuing money or retiring money, respectively, rather than by issuing or retiring interest-bearing government securities. The Myrdal proposal, known as the "Swedish budget," differs mainly in that it plans a cyclically balanced budget rather than a modest surplus over the cycle.

The "automatic" budget programs are open to similar criticisms. Their primary weakness is that although they do allow the

---

$3 billion in the 1947 document, while the 1961 document says it is probably something on the order of $3-7 billion.

[7] In terms of the graph (Figure XIII) used earlier to show a fiscal program, the CED proposal amounts to selecting a budget line such as A or B. Then if government spending increases, taxes must increase also, to keep the budget line in the same place and thus leave the surplus at high employment unchanged.

The CED proposal actually allows for changes in government spending unmatched by tax rate changes: (1) where the high employment surplus is growing because the GNP that produces 96 percent employment is growing due to increases in the labor force and its productivity; (2) where there is an urgent need for an extraordinary expenditure of a temporary nature; and (3) in the event of a severe economic depression or major inflation.

[8] "A Monetary and Fiscal Framework for Economic Stability," *American Economic Review* (June 1948), pp. 245-64, reprinted in *Essays in Positive Economics* (Univ. of Chicago Press, 1953), pp. 133-56.

[9] "Fiscal Policy in the Business Cycle," *American Economic Review* (March 1939), pp. 183-93, reprinted in *Readings in Fiscal Policy,* edited by Arthur Smithies and J. Keith Butters (Richard D. Irwin, Inc., 1955), pp. 291-306.

automatic stabilizers to stabilize the economy, that is, to reduce the magnitude of fluctuations in GNP, they do not necessarily stabilize it around the full employment level. Given government spending, as determined on a "needs" basis, only one particular level of tax rates at any period of time will generate full employment, and this level of tax rates (together with the given amount of government expenditures), may imply a surplus, a balanced budget, or a deficit at high (or full) employment. The goal of a moderate surplus or a balanced budget at full employment is not necessarily conducive to full employment. Where full employment can be achieved only with a planned deficit, a surplus or balanced budget will only frustrate the objective. Where full employment and stable prices are consistent only with a budget surplus, setting tax rates to produce a balanced budget, or too small a surplus, will tend to raise prices. There can be no rigidly fixed rules as to the proper surplus or deficit at full employment GNP, for this will vary as private demand varies.

A second facet of this problem is that changes in the world situation or domestic crises may call for substantial and frequent changes in government purchases of goods or services. Such events as the Korean War, Sputnik, Berlin, or the Cuban crisis, which cannot be predicted, may cause sharp changes in federal spending. Under the stabilizing budget proposals, each unexpected change would call for corresponding changes in tax rates, to keep the planned surplus at "high employment" the same.[10] Aside from the impracticability of trying to secure such tax changes from Congress every time a change in expenditures is required, the effect of equal increases in government spending and taxes at full employment GNP would not be neutral. Even without emergency changes, there would be a slow and probably continuous rise in government expenditures due to normal population growth and resulting demands for government services. If tax rates were raised correspondingly, the effect again would not be neutral. As government expenditures rise, the budget surplus at full employment GNP would have to be greater to keep the same fiscal impact. So the "rule" relating to the budget surplus at full

[10] Although the CED budget proposal allows for extraordinary changes in federal spending without tax rate changes, it confines these to "temporary" changes and in addition implies that they would not occur often. But they will occur often and in many cases will not be temporary.

employment GNP will in any case have to be continuously revised, which makes the "automatic budget" considerably less "automatic" and much more "discretionary."

These criticisms should not obscure the basic virtues of the automatic stabilizing budget proposals. They are unquestionably superior to the annually balanced budget as a guide to policy in that they recognize and accept the stabilizing effects of deficits and/or surpluses incurred as the automatic fiscal stabilizers operate over the course of a business cycle. Except for periods of chronically weak or excessive private demand and sharp changes in government spending, such a policy would probably produce reasonably good results. The chief danger is that a rule such as that calling for "a moderate surplus at high employment" may become too rigid in the minds of policymakers and be adhered to even when it is clearly inappropriate.

Formula Flexibility

Another version of automatic budget policy is the "formula flexibility" proposal, whereby tax rate changes (and perhaps changes in government expenditures) are legislated in advance, to occur automatically with changes in certain indexes of business activity. For example, legislation might provide for a tax cut to be made automatically if real GNP falls by a certain percentage; and for a tax rate increase to occur automatically when there is a certain percentage rise in GNP. Provisions like these would produce the same effects as do the automatic fiscal stabilizers.

This scheme has much that is appealing. It would avoid congressional delay in using tax rate changes as a stabilizing device and would add considerable potency to the fiscal arsenal. On the other hand, it would be difficult to implement in practice for two main reasons. First, price indexes and GNP data may at times give the wrong guidance, since they may reflect such temporary factors as strikes, crop failures, and others, which do not reflect basic underlying trends. Second, even if the required formulas could be worked out, it is unlikely that Congress would be willing to delegate its control over taxes to this extent. For this reason President Johnson has departed from previous recommendations for altering tax rates countercyclically. His latest suggestion is that Congress should modify its procedures to permit rapid action on temporary income tax cuts recommended by the President if recession threatens.[11]

Summary and Conclusions

Expenditures and receipts of the federal government, by virtue of their magnitude, are bound to have considerable impact on the economy. If they were programmed without an awareness of their overall impact, the effects could be disastrous; the federal government could create extensive unemployment or serious inflationary pressures.

This chapter has suggested that a workable fiscal program would be to fix the level of government purchases of goods and services on the basis of "need," to set tax rates so as to produce full employment GNP (with a given level of government expenditures) regardless of the resulting budget deficit or surplus, and to allow the automatic fiscal stabilizers to reduce the size of periodic swings of GNP around the full employment level.

Of the other fiscal programs examined, the concept of the annually balanced budget, it has been shown, would produce serious economic instability if put into practice. Proposals for fixing a goal of a certain budget surplus or deficit at full employment output and letting the automatic stabilizers work, have the merit of "fiscal discipline," but unfortunately impose rigid rules that are not necessarily best for many economic situations. Proposals for "formula flexibility" are probably too difficult to implement.

This discussion, however, implies a lack of concern on the part of the public over the possibility of continued deficits in time of slack private demand. But the public apparently *is* considerably exercised when planned deficits are incurred and the national debt increases. This leads to the question of the national debt and its relation to fiscal policy, which will be discussed in the next chapter.

[11] *Economic Report of the President* (1965), p. 11.

CHAPTER VII

Fiscal Policy and the National Debt

As WAS NOTED in the previous chapter, the federal government may have to run sizable deficits in times of weak private demand in order to raise planned spending to a high enough level to achieve full employment. This means that there may be prolonged periods of increasing national debt, with no assurance that better times will produce the surpluses required to offset the deficits.

It is precisely this possibility that exercises many critics of discretionary fiscal policy. In their view, increases in the national debt impose a burden on "future generations," aggravate inflationary tendencies, and threaten the nation's solvency. Their concern is voiced in statements such as the following by Senator John McClellan of Arkansas:

One of the greatest crimes of all . . . is one that is rarely considered by many Americans to be an offense at all . . .

The full effects of this crime will not likely fall upon the generation that is committing it, but may call for reckoning far in the future, and, unless the present trend is reversed, each succeeding generation will pay more heavily for it. The offense is being compounded annually, and its long-range effects are cause for serious alarm. This is the crime: the generation that controls the economy of this nation today and those who have important government responsibility are callously and mercilessly burdening the livelihood and earnings of the generation that will follow us with a tremendous oppressive national debt . . .

We are saddling our grandchildren . . . with the bills for our luxurious living. We have no moral right to do this . . .[1]

In contrast, consider this statement of the Council of Economic Advisers in connection with the 1963 tax cut proposal:

. . . under the present circumstances there is no reason to fear such increases in the public debt as tax reduction may entail. The ratio of interest payments on the debt to national income is small and is likely to fall, not rise. Nor is there any danger that the increase in the federal debt will be a burden on future generations. Tax reduction will increase investment, and hence the wealth we will bequeath, not decrease it. The danger is the opposite one. By failing to take expansionary fiscal action, we will keep both consumption and investment depressed, thus hurting not only ourselves, but future generations as well.[2]

Concern over the size and growth of the national debt is frequently reflected in actual or proposed congressional legislation. In 1959 two Texas Congressmen, Jim Wright and Frank Ikard, introduced a bill that would require that no less than 1 percent of the present debt be paid off annually until the entire debt was retired. Congress has long imposed a "ceiling" on the national debt and has shown considerable reluctance at times to raise it (while legislating the spending authority that makes the debt increase necessary).

Who is right? Is there or is there not a "burden" imposed by a national debt? Does the national debt lead to inflation and government bankruptcy? These questions are obviously crucial to the design of a fiscal program.

To simplify the issue, this discussion of the national debt is based on the assumption that all federal debt is held internally—by residents of the United States. This is not far from the actual situation, since currently more than 95 percent of federal debt is held domestically.

[1] "The Crime of National Insolvency," *Tax Review* (January 1964), pp. 2-3.
[2] *Economic Report of the President* (1963), p. 83.

TABLE 8. Federal Debt, December 1964

(In billions of dollars)

Item	Amount	
Public issues		265.6
Marketable	212.5	
Bills, certificates, and notes	115.5	
Treasury bonds	97.0	
Nonmarketable	53.1	
U. S. savings bonds	49.7	
Investment bonds	3.4	
Special issues[a]		46.1
Other		7.0
Total debt[b]		318.7

Source: *Economic Report of the President* (1965), p. 255.
[a] Issued to U. S. government investment accounts.
[b] Total includes noninterest-bearing debt, fully guaranteed securities, postal savings bonds, prewar bonds, adjusted service bonds, depository bonds, and armed forces leave bonds.

First a definition of the "national debt" is called for, a more controversial question than one might think. There follows a brief summary of data relating the growth of the national debt to other economic magnitudes. The next three sections deal with the issues surrounding the national debt: (1) the burden of the debt in a deficit setting resulting from attempts to alleviate unemployment by use of increased expenditures or reduced taxes; (2) the burden of the debt in a full employment setting; and (3) miscellaneous issues connected with the public debt, such as inflation, national solvency, etc.

Definition of the Public Debt

The federal debt or "national debt" consists of direct obligations or debts of the United States Treasury and obligations of federal government enterprises or agencies that are fully guaranteed by the Treasury. It is shown in Table 8, broken down by major category. There are "public issues" (that is, bonds, notes, and bills), which are generally sold to the public (some are held by federal agencies and trust funds), and "special issues," which are held only by government agencies and trust funds. Of "public issues," some are "marketable," that is, they are traded on securities markets, and some are "nonmarketable" and cannot be traded (for example,

United States Savings Bonds). They may, however, be redeemed in cash or converted into another issue.

This $318.7 billion is what is usually referred to as the "national debt," or "public debt." However, some writers, following Maurice Stans, have referred to a much larger figure of some $1 trillion as the "true" national debt of the government of the United States.[3] Stans obtained the $1 trillion total by adding $700-800 billion to the national debt to cover what he considered to be reasonably firm commitments of the federal government to *future* expenditures under existing federal plans, broken down as follows (rounded figures in billions of dollars):

Past Services:	
Civil Service retirement	$ 30
Military retirement	40
Veterans' program	300
Future Services:	
Unspent balances of prior year authorizations	40
Public assistance	50
Interstate highway system	30
Other (housing, public works, etc.)	30
Social Security benefits	250-300
Total	$770-820

There are several misconceptions and errors in this tabulation. The most important is that it is basically an error to consider planned future expenditures as a *debt* unless planned future *taxes* are also taken into account and matched against planned outlays. The result might indeed be a planned future *increase* in the debt, but it could just as well be a planned *reduction*. Even if it were assumed that Congress would not raise the necessary revenue to cover all of these spending commitments, only the uncovered amount would truly represent additional planned indebtedness of the federal government. In any case, future congressional action on taxes or on these spending commitments is impossible to predict, and any planned debt increase implied by such projections is at best a guess.

[3] Maurice Stans, Director of the Bureau of the Budget under President Eisenhower, in a syndicated column headed "Uncle Sam Faces $1 Trillion Debt," in the *Washington Post* (Feb. 19, 1962). This column has been widely quoted in newspaper editorials and columns.

This is not to say that awareness of such commitments for future spending is not important. It is for its tax rate implications if for no other reason. But it is misleading to call all future expenditures under existing programs a "debt" of the federal government.

Furthermore, the compilation contains other errors. In the case of the Social Security trust funds, no account is taken of future tax increases written into the current law, which would substantially reduce the "debt" figure. The highway expenditures figure also makes no allowance for receipts from the special taxes earmarked for the highway trust fund. Mr. Stans uses different concepts for different items: for example, the figure for veterans' benefits is an estimate of total future expenditures under existing laws, while the figure for the retirement systems represents net future liability discounted to present value.

The principal causes of the growth of our public debt have been wars and depressions. During World War I the public debt rose sharply by about $22 billion to a level of $25.5 billion in 1919. From there it *decreased* some $9 billion to $16.2 billion in 1930. The economic depression of the thirties led to government deficit spending, and the public debt increased by approximately $27 billion between June 1929 and June 1940. During World War II it grew tremendously, reaching $269.4 billion at the end of 1946. Since 1946 the debt has continued to grow, especially during years of recession, and it stood at $318.7 billion in December 1964.[4]

Data on the Public Debt

Merely looking at the growth of the debt in isolation reveals little except that it has grown tremendously (4,000 times over) over the years the United States government has been in existence, from $75 million in 1791 to about $319 billion as of December 1964. But so have other economic measures, in particular the volume of output and private debts. Likewise federal interest payments

[4] A substantial amount of this debt is held by the Federal Reserve System ($37 billion) and by government investment accounts ($60.6 billion). For purposes of eonomic analysis, the net public debt held by the public, rather than the gross debt, is the relevant figure. For more discussion and detail on the growth of the public debt, see Marshall A. Robinson, *The National Debt Ceiling, An Experiment in Fiscal Policy* (Brookings Institution, 1959), pp. 20-25.

have grown immensely over the 175 years of our existence as a nation, but so has our ability to carry them.

To get some perspective on the growth of the national debt, it is useful to make the comparisons shown in Figures XIV-XVI. Figure XIV shows, for five-year intervals since 1900, the ratio of the gross national debt to GNP (in current dollars).[5] The debt-GNP ratio was very low up to 1916, rose sharply during World War I, and declined through the 1920's. It then rose during the 1930's and World War II and has fallen since, and it is currently back almost to the levels that prevailed in the middle and late 1930's. In Figure XV the growth of federal debt is compared with the growth of nonfederal debt since 1900. A comparison of the lines on the chart shows clearly that federal debt grew faster than nonfederal debt during the periods 1917-19 and 1930-45, but that in the other 45 years of the 63-year period, nonfederal debt grew faster.[6]

Finally, Figure XVI shows interest paid on the federal debt, both in dollars and as a percentage of GNP. Since 1900, interest paid on the federal debt has not exceeded 2.5 percent of GNP—a level reached just after World War II. The percentage fell to 1.7 by 1957 and is now just under 2 percent. The growth of federal debt, then, though large in absolute terms, appears less awesome when related to the growth of output or of private debt.

The Burden of the Debt: Unemployment Setting

As was noted at the outset, hostility to the size of the national debt as well as to its growth generally reflects the view that it imposes a burden on future generations. Consider first a society where there is unemployment, and assume that the government plans to run a deficit to finance additional expenditures or cuts in taxes in order to restore output to a full employment level. The issue then is

---

[5] It should be noted that a considerable portion of the federal debt is held as an asset by agencies of the federal government, and that the "publicly held debt" is much smaller than the gross debt. At the end of 1964, for example, the gross federal debt was $318.7 billion, while the net or publicly held debt was but $221.1 billion.

[6] Because the vertical axes are a ratio scale, the slopes or "steepness" of the lines show the rates of growth of public and private debt.

FIGURE XIV. Gross Federal Debt, Five-Year Intervals, 1900–30, Annually, 1931–64

Billions of Dollars

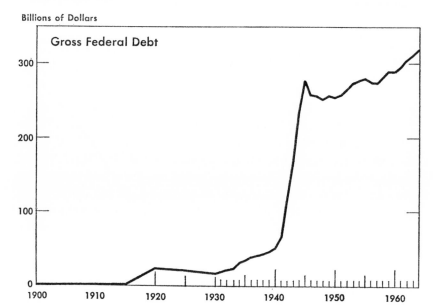

Sources: *Economic Report of the President* (1964), p. 271; 1900–25, R. G. Goldsmith, *A Study of Savings in the United States* (Princeton Univ. Press, 1955), Vol. I, p. 985.

Percent of GNP

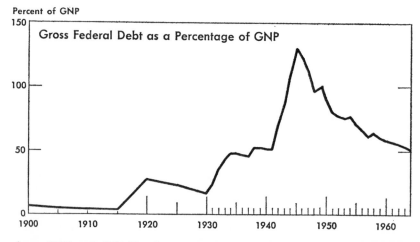

Sources: GNP figures for 1956–64 are from *Economic Report of the President* (1965), p. 189; for 1919–55 from U. S. Department of Commerce, Bureau of the Census, *Historical Statistics of the United States, Colonial Times to 1957*, p. 139; for 1900–18 from Goldsmith, *op. cit.*, Vol. 3, p. 427.

FIGURE XV. Federal and Non-Federal Debt, 1900–63

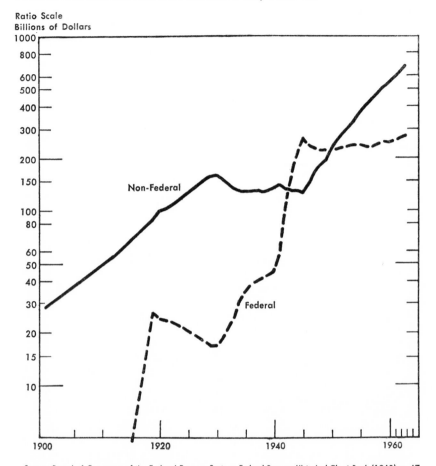

Ratio Scale
Billions of Dollars

Source: Board of Governors of the Federal Reserve System, *Federal Reserve Historical Chart Book* (1963), p. 67

whether or not a burden on future generations is implied when the government borrows to finance the planned deficit.

In one sense at least, there is clearly no burden on later generations. *A closed society cannot dispose of more goods and services than it currently produces; it cannot borrow tomorrow's output today.* In a period of unemployment there is essentially no competition between the government and the private sector for resources. Goods and services acquired by the government at the time of the expenditure do not reduce the output available to consumers or private investors. In fact, as was seen in Chapter 5, there would be

FIGURE XVI. Gross Interest Paid on Federal Debt, Five-Year Intervals, 1900–30, Annually, 1931–64

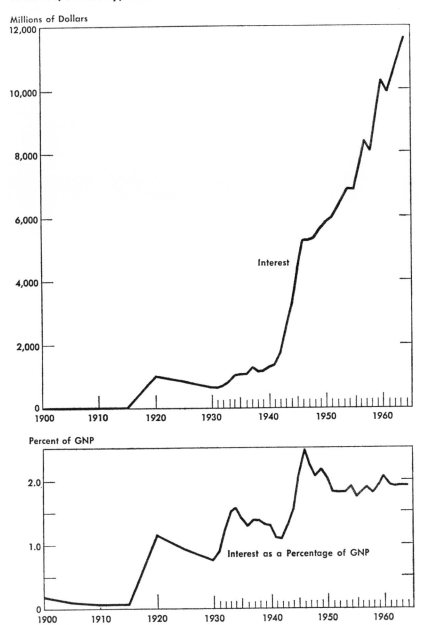

Millions of Dollars

Percent of GNP

Interest

Interest as a Percentage of GNP

Sources: Data for 1958-64 from U. S. Department of Commerce, *Survey of Current Business* (several issues); for 1951-57, U. S. Department of Commerce, *U. S. Income and Output*, 1958, p. 164; for 1930–50, U. S. Department of Commerce, *National Income* (1954), pp. 172–73; for 1900–25, Goldsmith, op. cit., Vol. 3, p. 445.

some "multiplier effect" tending to increase *both* private investment and consumption if government spending were increased or taxes were cut. In short, deficit financing to restore full employment would make future generations better off to the extent that private investment was thus stimulated, for in the absence of the expenditure increase or the tax cut, the added investment would not take place, and future generations would have a smaller private capital stock and lower output. There is a further gain in future output resulting from government spending of an investment type, for example, for schools, bridges, roads, etc.

What about the interest payments and possibly the repayment of the principal on the debt that falls to the lot of future generations. Is this not a burden? The answer is "no." There is no aggregate burden on future generations who have to make interest payments on the debt and perhaps repay the principal, for these are simply *transfers* of income (or wealth) among members of society. There may indeed be "distributional effects"—wealth will be redistributed from taxpayers to bondholders to the extent that these are not the same individuals, but this does not necessarily leave the community "worse off" in the aggregate. In summary, deficit finance and increases in the national debt do not impose a burden on future generations in an unemployment setting. Running deficits to promote full employment leaves future generations better off in terms of increased real output and investment. In this case, at least, inter-generation equity is not violated if a deficit is incurred to eliminate unemployment.[7]

[7] Franco Modigliani has developed a somewhat different argument on this question. He reasons that under certain conditions a deficit created to boost the economy from a depression or recession *can* leave future generations worse off than if no government action were taken. Suppose recessions or depressions are "temporary," that is, that the economy will recover eventually even if no government action is taken. Suppose further that consumers and firms together have a plan of desired capital accumulation. The recession then will reduce the present generation's capital below the desired level, since saving and investment are reduced as income falls. The reduction in the present generation's capital below what it would have been will force them to cut their consumption over their lifetime (even after full employment is restored) to an extent equal to the loss in the accumulation of capital during the period of unemployment. In short, they save more to accumulate the capital "lost" during the recession. The higher rate of capital formation after full employment is restored will tend to build the stock of capital back to where it would have been without the temporary unemployment, by the time the recession generation disappears. On the other hand, if the gov-

The Burden of the Debt: Full Employment Setting

Now consider a society that is always at full employment regardless of what the government does or does not do as to spending, taxes, and the like. Assume that the government plans to spend an additional $100. Will it make any difference, in terms of a burden on future generations, if that expenditure is debt-financed or tax-financed?

If full employment is assumed, goods and services acquired by the government must always be "paid for" by a reduction in the output available to the private sector at the time of the expenditure. So, whether tax-financed or debt-financed, the expenditures by the government cannot possibly be "paid for" by future generations; there is no burden on them in this sense.

As far as servicing interest payments and possibly the repayment of the principal on the debt go, here too, as in the unemployment case, no burden is imposed on future generations in the aggregate. These are simply transfers of income (or wealth) among members of society.

However, while it is true that a closed community cannot increase today's output by borrowing tomorrow's, how today's output is used can affect the output of tomorrow, and debt-financing has a different impact on the use of today's output than does tax-financing of an expenditure. This point provides the explanation for whatever real "burden" might be imposed on future generations by debt-financing of an expenditure.

If the economy is at full employment, then, by definition, the increase in government spending cannot increase total output. Prices will rise whether the increase in government spending is debt-

---

ernment acts to combat the recession and creates new debt in doing so, the new debt to some extent replaces the "lost" capital in the net worth of investors. Thus the present generation does not seek to build the capital stock back to what it would have been; it is content with government bonds rather than physical capital. Later generations may thus have less private capital than if the government had not attacked the recession by running a deficit.

Of course, the crux of this argument is the assumption that recessions are in fact "temporary," as well as the assumptions about the productivity of government expenditures. See his article "Long-Run Implications of Alternative Fiscal Policies and the Burden of the National Debt," *Economic Journal* (December 1961), p. 731.

financed or tax-financed. But how is investment affected? Suppose an increase in government spending of $100 is debt-financed. Taxes on private income, and therefore private disposable (after-tax) income, will be unchanged. Assuming that private consumption depends only on the level of disposable personal income of consumers, and that private investment depends only on interest rates (credit conditions), then consumption of private goods will remain unchanged. Because consumption outlays are unaffected, the decrease in private use of output must (according to our assumptions) fall on private investment. Debt-financing of an expenditure, then, will tend to result in a fall in private investment by the amount of the increase in government spending.[8]

How does the result in this case compare with that in the case of a like amount of tax-financed expenditure? In the latter case, some part of the tax increase will come out of private personal income. Private consumption will decline by some fraction of the reduction in disposable personal income that is occasioned by the increase in taxes, since, as was noted earlier, consumers in the aggregate do not consume all of any increase in disposable personal income. The balance of the impact will fall then on private investment. This means that both private consumption and investment will fall, with the total decline in both being just equal to the total increase in government spending.

Comparing the two cases, it is clear that, although investment falls in both the debt-financed and tax-financed cases, it falls more in the former. Here lies the "burden" of debt-financing. The burden on future generations is measured in terms of the loss of potential output associated with the loss of potential private capital. That is, debt-financing will reduce private investment more than will tax-financing of the same amount of expenditure, thereby leaving future generations with less capital equipment to produce with and thus restricting them to a lower level of private output. Both debt-financing and tax-financing leave future generations with less private capital and thus less output. However, debt-financing leaves them relatively worse off.

[8] Under different assumptions debt-financing need not lead to a fall in private investment by an amount equal to the increase in government spending. It may in part reduce consumer credit rather than investment credit.

Nothing has been said thus far about the use to which the government expenditure is put, and government outlays have implicitly been assumed to be unproductive. But government expenditures are not unproductive. They may be less, or more, "productive" than private investment. If government expenditure is less productive than, or equally as productive as, private investment, these conclusions about the relative burden still hold. If, however, the government expenditure is more productive, future generations will be better off with the government expenditure than without it, whether it is debt-financed or tax-financed. But they will be relatively less well off with debt-financing than with tax-financing. There is still a "burden" in the full employment setting in debt-financing relative to tax-financing, in the sense that the gain to future generations is less.[9]

In summary, deficit financing and increases in the national debt do not necessarily impose an absolute burden on future generations in the full employment setting. If government expenditures are more productive than is private investment, future generations will be better off with the debt-financed expenditures than without such expenditures. However, there is still a relative burden: future generations would benefit relatively more from such expenditures if they were financed by increasing taxes rather than by increasing the federal debt.

In any event, since the federal government ordinarily runs surpluses when the economy is at full employment, the likelihood of

[9] Some economists, notably E. J. Mishan, dispute the validity of the argument that a burden is imposed on future generations by borrowing rather than taxing, even in a full employment setting. Mishan argues that since taxes reduce present consumption and borrowing reduces private capital for future generations, if one talks about a burden being imposed on future generations by borrowing, there is an equal obligation to consider the burden imposed on the present generation by taxing. Every decision society undertakes today will affect future generations. Thus decisions to debt-finance government expenditure are no more of a burden on future generations than are decisions by individuals to consume rather than to invest. "After all, we could enormously increase provision for the future if we preferred heroic feats of austerity during our lifetime. Are we then not imposing a heavy burden on the future generation to the extent that we eschew their heroic feats of austerity and instead follow the path of our wonted self-indulgence?" ("How to Make a Burden of the Public Debt," *Journal of Political Economy* [December 1963], p. 540.)

imposing burdens on future generations through debt financing is small.

Deficits and Other Issues

Some newspaper and magazine writers and pamphleteers make categorical statements to the effect that "the increasing debt (deficit) is inflationary," linking together hostility to deficits and an increasing national debt and the general desire to avoid inflation. But as has already been noted in Chapter 6, the deficit, or the "full employment deficit," is not a reliable measure of fiscal policy. A large actual deficit can result from a very anti-inflationary fiscal policy if the government "tightens up" too much and induces a recession, or if expenditures drop in the private sector, the economy goes into a recession, and federal tax receipts fall as GNP declines. Large deficits occurred in the 1940's during a period of high employment and upward price pressure (which was suppressed by price and wage controls). During the period 1931-34, however, large deficits occurred during a period of severe unemployment and falling prices. There is no basis for measuring the inflationary or deflationary impact of federal fiscal action by the actual deficit or surplus.

It is often implied that all inflation is due to higher federal outlays, or that private and state-local outlays are not inflationary but federal government outlays are. It is said too that private or state and local government outlays are productive whereas federal government outlays are "unproductive." GNP is said to be a faulty measure of a nation's output, primarily because it includes in total output these "unproductive" government purchases of goods and services.

Such arguments show a faulty understanding of what determines a nation's output, the causes of inflation or depression, and the nature of output. If government purchases of goods and services were "unproductive," society might just as well discontinue such outlays and use the resources thus freed in the private sector. It could eliminate expenditures on missiles, planes, courts, police, highways, and education and use the resources to produce more cars, electric shavers, houses, and private planes. Obviously, federal (as well as state and local) government expenditures *are* "productive." They satisfy certain social needs as determined by elected representatives, who are responsible to the electorate.

It is clear also that increases in private outlays for consumption and investment can at times be responsible for inflationary pressures, as they were in the period 1946-48. Whether private or government spending is at the root of inflation, the important thing is to bring about a reduction in aggregate spending.

The Public Debt and National Bankruptcy

There is a great deal of emotion in people's attitudes toward the public debt. For example, statements are frequently made to the effect that if the national debt reaches some particular level, the government's credit standing will be impaired, and disaster will follow in the form of something casually referred to as "national bankruptcy." While it is difficult to evaluate these statements, the idea that there is a definite limit to the size of the national debt that can be carried without disaster is not a new one. Individuals have long predicted that a debt of one-tenth, one-fifth, or one-half of the amount we now have would result in national bankruptcy, and they have revised the limit upward when it was indeed passed and ruin failed to ensue.

How much *can* the federal government borrow? Is there a point beyond which borrowing would have to cease because people would refuse to lend? To answer this, one must understand the basis for the credit standing of governments, whether federal, state, or local. Governments have a power not shared by other borrowers —they can impose taxes with which to pay interest on their debt and repay the principal. As long as a government does not abuse its taxing power, it will have the ability to borrow. It may have to pay higher interest charges if its debt becomes quite large, but it can borrow as long as it is willing to do so. And this is not all; central governments also have the power to coin and print money. They can always do this, instead of imposing taxes, to meet interest costs on their debts, and as long as they do so, they can continue to borrow.

As a matter of fact, the securities of the United States Treasury are looked on by investors as a nearly riskless investment (from the standpoint of defaulting on interest payments), despite the enormous increase in the debt in the last half century.

This does not mean that we should not worry about deficits and the growth of the debt. If the debt is growing because private demand is weak and the government is pursuing a policy of stimulating the economy with tax reduction (or expenditure increases), the deficit is not only harmless but a benefit to the health of the economy. If private spending is strong, however, and prices are rising, then low tax rates and a deficit are poor policy indeed. In short, there are good deficits and bad deficits. Good deficits occur as fiscal policy is used to stimulate the economy or to cushion it against economic declines. Bad deficits occur when, in the face of strong private spending, government refuses to raise taxes (given the desired government expenditures) to eliminate inflationary pressure.

The Psychological Effects

It has been held that even though there may be no danger of burdening future generations, the stimulative effects of increasing the public debt to counteract recessions may be negated or partially offset by the unwarranted public hostility to debt increases. That is, irrational fear of such increases may reduce private spending (particularly investment), which will offset the stimulative effect of the fiscal action producing the deficit. Businessmen may say "with such fiscal irresponsibility in the White House I will not commit my company to new capital outlays."

On the other hand, the "announcement effects" of stimulative federal fiscal actions may be quite the opposite. The stock market's reaction to tax cut suggestions in 1963, and comments in the business press, suggest that such positive fiscal action actually encourages business optimism and stimulates investment.

There is no clear answer as to which effect is likely to be dominant. It is hard to single out the effect on businessmen's expectations of a single action of an administration, such as incurring a planned deficit. It is probably true that the overall image of an administration has an important psychological influence on business investment decisions. It is not clear what influence a deficit by itself has, or how strong that influence may be.

Summary and Conclusions

From the discussion in this chapter, it is clear that deficits may be economically defensible and even desirable under a great many conditions. They are unjustified, of course, when the economy is fully employed and there are inflationary pressures. If deficits are incurred as part of a rounded program to restore full employment, they are all to the good. They tend to increase output and employment and impose no identifiable real burden on future generations. Future interest payments and the repayment of principal are essentially financial transfers involving no aggregate real burden. Arguments to the effect that increasing federal debt will somehow lead to national ruin or bankruptcy have little foundation in fact. And while there may be adverse psychological effects from deficits, there may just as well be salutary ones.

CHAPTER VIII

Determining the Need for Federal Spending

THE AMOUNT OF FEDERAL expenditures and taxes needed has been shown to depend, at least in part, on the state of the economy. When private demand for goods and services is weak, federal taxes should be adjusted downward, or expenditures should be increased, or both. When private demand is strong, stabilization may call for restraint in expenditures, or higher tax rates, or both.

Clearly, however, federal expenditures must also be judged on other grounds besides their effects on employment, prices, and growth. Production of nuclear submarines, the number of defense personnel, or defense research cannot readily be adjusted up or down as private demand weakens or becomes buoyant. Nor can old age pensions and retirement benefits under social security be juggled to offset ups or downs in private spending, although the timing of payments can be accelerated when necessary. Interest payments on the federal debt, highway construction, and public health are other examples of federal programs that are difficult to vary for counter-cyclical reasons. While the total amount of spending may be evaluated with an eye to the current state of the economy and this will in turn affect budget decisions on particular programs, the basis for judging individual federal spending programs cannot be solely, or even primarily, their impact on the level of economic activity.

What other criteria are or should be used? What can the citizen use, apart from the stabilization criteria, as a basis for determining whether the proposed levels of spending or the amounts to be spent on different programs are "proper"? Certainly people do have views on these matters, as editorial pages, letters to editors, and casual conversations clearly indicate. They may complain about "wild-eyed spenders," or deplore the neglect of certain federal programs, or both. Yet if individuals are pressed to explain their views about federal spending proposals, it often seems that they have few objective criteria for judging the "need" for federal spending. They may defend a particular program by saying it will "help the community," "create jobs," "meet human needs," or "keep (my) industry prosperous." Programs may be attacked as "unnecessary," "involving a concentration of power in Washington," "better left to the local community," or "profligate and wasteful."

This chapter investigates the issue of federal spending criteria other than stabilization policy.

Purposes of Federal Spending

The basic data are presented in Table 9, where 1963 federal expenditures are classified according to function and type (transfer payments, grants-in-aid, etc.). Several features of federal expenditures shown in this table should be noted. Out of total federal spending of about $115 billion, only some $65 billion represent purchases of goods and services. Transfer payments—involving not payment for services but for old age benefits, retirement benefits, etc.—account for $30 billion, and interest paid on the debt is over $7 billion. Another $9.1 billion represent grants-in-aid to state and local governments.

The functional breakdown of federal expenditures discloses some interesting facts. First, the importance of defense spending is obvious; it accounts for half of total federal expenditures. Second, it may be surprising to some to find that old age and retirement benefit payments by the federal government account for about one-eighth of total federal spending. If net interest payments of $7.7 billion are added to national defense expenditures and old age and retirement benefits, these items alone account for three-fourths of total federal spending—some $81 billion in 1963. All the other programs of the federal government—foreign aid, agriculture, natural resources, transportation, veterans' benefits, and public assistance—make up only one-fourth of total federal spending.

How can one decide what the federal government *should* do in each of these areas?

Federal vs. State-Local Responsibility

One very basic issue regarding the need for federal spending is: Should the responsibility for a particular program rest with the federal government or with the states and their subdivisions?

The legal division of responsibility among the various levels of government is found in the Constitution and in court interpretations of it. The Constitution divided the powers of government, those of the national government being specified (Article I, Section VIII), while those of the states and their subdivisions are residual. The tenth amendment reserves to the states all powers not granted to the national government.[1] The federal government (through Congress) was given the power "to levy and collect taxes, duties, imposts, and excises, to pay the debts, and provide for the common defense and general welfare of the United States," which was intended to severely restrict the scope of federal activity. There is no specific mention of spending for highways, public health, education, or public welfare, here or anywhere else in the Constitution; and since the tenth amendment does not deny these powers to the states, it may be presumed that they are residual powers of the states.

Until the 1930's the courts were very reluctant to allow the national government to assume powers beyond providing for national defense and regulating interstate trade and commerce, and the Congress was generally reluctant to seek more responsibilities. As a result, in 1927 the federal government provided less than one-fifth of total government expenditures for civilian purposes—17 percent.[2]

However, during the decade of the 1930's, with the problems and pressures of the greatest economic depression in United States history, there developed a shift in social philosophy and judicial

[1] James A. Maxwell, *Financing State and Local Governments* (Brookings Institution, 1965), Chap. I.

[2] *Ibid.*

TABLE 9. Federal Expenditures by Function, 1963

(*Dollar amounts in billions*)

Item	Purchases of goods and services	Transfer payments and net interest paid	Grants-in-aid to state and local governments	Subsidies less current surplus of government enterprises	Total[a]	Percentage of total[a]
(1)						
National defense	55.2	2.0	0.5	−0.1	57.6	50.0
General government, except net interest paid	2.1	1.3		−0.1	3.3	2.8
International affairs finances	0.9	1.6			2.5	2.1
Subtotal	58.2	4.9	0.5	−0.2	63.4	55.1
(2)						
Public assistance and relief			2.9		2.9	2.5
Old age and retirement benefits	0.2	16.4			16.6	14.4
Other social security and special welfare	0.4		0.2		0.6	0.5
Labor and manpower	0.2		0.5		0.7	0.6
Veterans' service and benefits	1.4	4.7			6.1	5.2
Agriculture and agric. resources	0.3		0.2	3.3	3.9	3.3
Unemployment benefits paid		2.9			2.9	2.5
Housing and community development			0.2		0.2	0.2
Subtotal	2.5	24.0	4.0	3.3	33.9	29.3
(3)						
Public health and sanitation	0.6	0.8	0.3		1.6	1.5
Education	0.4	0.2	0.6		1.1	0.9
Transportation	1.2		3.5	0.3	5.0	4.3
Postal services	0.1			0.5	0.6	0.5
Natural resources	2.3		0.1	−0.2	2.3	1.9
Subtotal	4.6	1.0	4.5	0.6	10.6	9.3
(4)						
Net interest paid		7.7			7.7	6.7
Government sales	−0.8				−0.8	
Subtotal	−0.8	7.7			6.9	5.9
Total expenditures	64.7	37.6	9.1	3.8	115.2	100.0

Source: U. S. Department of Commerce, *Survey of Current Business* (July 1964), p. 21.
[a] Details may not add to totals because of rounding.

thinking. The judicial interpretation of the Constitution that emerged in the 1930's "accepted a reading of the general welfare clause that places no discernible judicial limits on the amounts or purposes of federal spending. . . ."[3] During this period the federal share of civilian expenditures rose to 42 percent (1938), and it has remained above 35 percent since that time.[4] In short, the powers of the national government to tax and spend have become very broad and now cover many areas of spending formerly reserved exclusively for the states and their subdivisions, for example, public welfare, relief, public health, etc. Thus there are generally no precise legal boundaries to the areas of responsibility of the various levels of government.[5]

The division of responsibility among levels of government with regard to spending and taxation is now a question mainly for legislative-executive judgment. Such a judgment generally revolves around at least two criteria. One of these is efficiency. In determining federal programs, Congress and the President nearly always consider whether or not the program can be carried out most efficiently at the federal level or at some other level. Some activities, such as sewage treatment and garbage disposal, can clearly be carried out most efficiently at the local level. Some, such as policing of highway traffic, can be most efficiently carried out by state governments. Others, like national defense and postal service, can achieve the greatest economies when undertaken by the federal government. Aside from these cases, about which there is little dispute, there is a host of activities, such as education, medical care for the aged, public health, and highway construction, where there may be pronounced differences of opinion as to which level can most efficiently provide the service. In any case, virtually all proposals for federal as against state-local spending are judged in part on the question of efficiency.

Another criterion is political. Undue expansion of federal activity is feared because individual freedom, liberty, and political activity are best preserved by keeping government activities at the lowest level possible, that is, by emphasizing decentralization.

---

[3] See Maxwell, *op. cit.,* and Commission on Intergovernmental Relations, *A Report to the President* (1955), p. 29.

[4] *Ibid.*

[5] There are exceptions to this statement. For example, the provision of police protection is a responsibility still reserved to the states.

Keeping government activity at the lowest level possible may make for closer contact among the persons receiving the services, those paying the taxes, and the government officials who make policy and administer the programs. Transfer of these activities, or portions of them, to higher government levels may mean that decisions are being made by government officials not familiar with the circumstances, needs, and desires of those affected.

The two criteria—efficiency and decentralization—often conflict. A particular program might be most efficient if administered at the federal level but might also create, in the minds of many persons, an undesirable, additional concentration of power at that level. In such cases the public, through their elected representatives, must choose. There is no way to say which criterion—efficiency or decentralization—should be given more weight.

However, suppose, for the purposes of this chapter, that the crucial issue of the division of responsibility between the federal government and the states is resolved. That is, suppose the federal government has certain clearly defined areas of responsibility, for example national defense. In this setting, then, how big should the federal budget be? How much should the federal government spend on national defense? Agriculture? Old-age assistance?

Spending on Public Goods

Consider the federal spending programs in group (1) in Table 9, that is, national defense, general government (except net interest) and international affairs. This group of federal expenditures amounted to $63.4 billion in 1963. Of this total, $58.2 billion was for purchases of goods and services, and $4.9 billion was for transfer payments. Grants-in-aid and subsidies less current surplus of government enterprises were negligible.

As Table 9 shows, this type accounted for 55 percent of total federal expenditures in 1963. This large portion of federal spending is clearly on certain kinds of goods and services which, if they are not provided by government, will not be provided at all. As Adam Smith put it almost three hundred years ago: "those public institutions and those public works, which though they may be in the highest degree advantageous to a great society, are, however, of such a nature, that the profits could never repay the expense to any individual or small number of individuals."[6]

These goods and services are usually referred to as "public goods." The most common characteristic of public goods is their availability to all individuals independently of each individual's tax contributions. Probably the best example of this is national defense. Every United States citizen benefits to some degree from the security provided by defense regardless of what share of the cost he may bear. Also, the use by any one individual or group of individuals of the public good or service, such as national defense, will not reduce the amount available for any other individual or group of individuals. This is not true of most private goods. Since the benefits resulting from public goods accrue to society as a whole, a market price for sales of units of the service cannot possibly be established. Who would provide nuclear submarines and Army divisions if the federal government did not? Public goods are usually financed through general taxation.

To determine how much of those public goods for which the federal government is responsible should be produced, and thus how much should be spent on them by the federal government, something other than a price system must be used. Since public goods yield certain benefits to society and also impose certain costs on it, a comparison of such benefits and costs might be a useful criterion.[7]

Unfortunately the task of estimating society's benefits and costs from additional units of many types of federal government expenditure is difficult. As an example, consider defense expenditures again. How can one estimate the additional benefits to society from

---

[6] Adam Smith, *The Wealth of Nations* (Random House, Modern Library Edition, 1937), p. 68.

[7] Cost-benefit analysis has been applied in certain fields of federal spending where at least a rough estimation of society's benefits and costs is possible. Specific examples of federal projects subjected to cost-benefit estimates are irrigation, flood control, water-pollution control, and power projects. For discussions of several cost-benefit analyses and reference to others, see John V. Krutilla and Otto Eckstein, *Multiple Purpose River Development* (Johns Hopkins Press, 1958); Otto Eckstein, *Water Resource Development* (Harvard Univ. Press, 1958); Charles J. Hitch and Roland N. McKean, *The Economics of Defense in the Nuclear Age* (Harvard Univ. Press, 1960). For recent attempts to apply cost-price analysis to other government programs, see Robert Dorfman, ed., *Measuring Benefits of Government Investments* (Brookings Institution, 1965).

additional units of defense, such as one more nuclear submarine than the number we already have? The cost to society of providing an additional nuclear submarine is the additional quantity of other private or public goods and services (refrigerators, television sets or police protection, water pollution control, flood control, etc.) that is given up in order to provide the nuclear submarine. As important as certain private and public goods may be—say, water pollution control—there is no way to tell whether society's benefits from an additional unit of nuclear submarine exceed or fall short of society's costs in giving up a certain amount of water pollution control.

Since neither additional benefits nor costs of many large programs can be measured in any meaningful way (at least at present), the cost-benefit criterion offers little guidance in determining the size of the federal budget for public goods. As Walter Heller put it:

The economist recognizes, of course, that there are areas where he is necessarily mute, or at least should not speak unless spoken to. These are the area of pure public goods, whose benefits are clearly indivisible and nonmarketable, and no amount of economic wisdom can determine the appropriate levels of output and expenditure. In the realm of defense, for example, one successful Russian earth satellite or intercontinental ballistics missile will (and should) outweigh 10,000 economists in determining the appropriate level of expenditures.[8]

Spending to Affect Income Distribution

Federal government spending and taxation also arise out of efforts to promote equity in the distribution of income among persons and regions. The federal expenditures in group (2) of Table 9 were designed primarily for this purpose. As can be seen from the table, this type of spending bulks very large in the federal budget. It represented some 29 percent of total expenditures in 1963. Of the $33.9 billion of federal spending on the items in category (2), $24 billion was in the form of transfer payments, $4.0 billion was for grants-in-aid to state and local governments (mostly for public assistance and relief), $3.3 billion was for subsidies (less current surplus of government enterprises) and, finally, $2.5 billion represented purchases of goods and services.

[8] Walter W. Heller, "Economics and the Applied Theory of Public Expenditures," in *Federal Expenditure Policy for Economic Growth and Stability*, U.S. Congress, Joint Economic Committee, 85 Cong. 1 sess., p. 103.

In our society, government spending and taxation affect the distribution of income in two ways: First, when government taxes and spends, it usually alters in some way the distribution of income regardless of whether or not it had such an objective in mind. When government, for example, awards a contract to a business firm to build submarines, its primary objective is a stronger defense posture. Nevertheless, this expenditure, and the way in which it is financed, probably will have some effect on the distribution of income. The business firm to which the contract is awarded, as well as its suppliers of materials, labor, etc., will benefit directly in terms of work opportunities, income, and profits from the government expenditure.

Second, certain programs of spending and taxation are designed specifically to affect the distribution of income. These are the ones listed in group (2) of Table 9. Federal government spending on public housing, agriculture, public hospitals, medical services, old age and retirement benefits, veterans' benefits, public assistance, and relief is undertaken especially for the benefit of certain individuals or groups, mostly poor people or those in distress circumstances for economic or other reasons. The benefits derived from these specific programs may accrue to all individuals in the society, but the important aspect of this type of spending is that particular groups of individuals (the aged, the disabled, veterans, farmers, etc.) benefit more than others. With respect to taxation, the government may design a specific tax structure (a combination of certain income, gift, death, and other tax rates) to influence the distribution of income.[9]

It would probably be inaccurate to say that the Executive Branch or the majority of Congress has any considered overall view of what the distribution of income should be. Nevertheless, decisions on specific proposals, such as those listed above, all involve implicit judgments on a desirable distribution of income. Unanimity of opinion about what is "fair" or "equitable" may be impossible to attain in a given society, and "fairness" does not necessarily mean the same thing for every society at every moment of time. What is considered unfair today may have been regarded as fair in earlier

---

[9] Alternatively, the government may interfere directly (not through spending or taxation) in the determination of income in the private market by imposing minimum wages or minimum prices for certain services or products.

times. Nevertheless, some general distributional patterns are probably supported by a majority, and fairly general agreement may be reached on many specific cases.

Given a goal of a particular pattern of income distribution, federal government transfers and taxes will be set to achieve that goal. That is, given (1) the initial allocation of wealth and income generated by private markets and (2) the effects on distribution of federal government spending and taxing for other purposes, such as to allocate resources to the production of public goods, there will be some amount of government transfers and taxes required to achieve any desired income distribution. How much will depend on what the desired distribution is and how different from it the distribution pattern would be without any taxes or transfers.

Spending on Semi-Public Goods

Consider the federal expenditures grouped together in (3) of Table 9. This $10.6 billion represents expenditures on what may be called semi-public goods. This type of spending is relatively small at the federal level (accounting for only 9 percent of federal expenditures in 1963), but is a very large part of state-local government expenditures. Semi-public goods are goods and services whose benefits to individual users are less than the total benefit derived from them by society. Take, for example, the case of education, which yields a direct benefit to the user in the form of a higher expected life income. However, as in the case of a public good, education provides additional benefits to society as a whole, for example, better environment for innovations, more qualified voters, better health, a reduction in the crime rate, etc. Such a semi-public good can be supplied to individual users by private producers in the free market economy, as in the case of private schools and colleges. But since education provides extra benefits to society, the government may be called upon to supplement the amount of education supplied by the private market.

Education as a semi-public good is provided mostly by the state-local governments, in the form of public schools, colleges, and universities. The federal government, however, contributes to state and local government spending on education through its grants-in-aid. As Table 9 shows, 50 percent of federal spending on education is in that form. In addition, the federal government provides aid to education for areas affected by federal installations, loans and grants to college students, and other services. Various bills have been introduced in recent years to extend federal aid in the area of education to construction, teachers' salaries, and other costs. Opinions on these bills have generally revolved around the alternatives of efficiency versus decentralization discussed earlier.

To determine how much the federal government should spend on the semi-public goods for which it, rather than state-local governments, has been given responsibility, the benefits accruing to the individual and those received by the community must both be identified. For example, a multi-purpose river development program would provide benefits for individuals and for the community as a whole from the production of electric power, fertilizers, flood control, etc. If the total benefits exceeded the cost, the project would be "worthwhile." If not, it should not be undertaken. In this field of water resources development, cost-benefit analysis has been applied successfully. But in others, such as education, public health, and sanitation, such estimates are not yet possible, and little use has been made of cost-benefit analysis to determine the size of federal spending in these areas.

Other Federal Spending

The fourth group in Table 9 consists of net interest paid and government sales of goods and services produced by government enterprises. The largest and most important item in this group is net interest. Interest paid on its debt to the public by the federal government in 1963 accounted for 6.7 percent of federal government expenditures. Since the debt was incurred mostly as the result of past wars and recessions, it has something of the character of a defense expenditure or of an expenditure that represents in part the cost to the government of stabilizing the economy.

Some Common Fallacies in Judging Federal Spending

There are uncomfortably few criteria that can be used to determine the optimum level of federal expenditures and taxation because the nature of many government goods and services is such that their benefits and costs cannot readily be measured. One frequent argument is that all increases in federal (or other) government spending should be opposed, because by its very nature government is less efficient than the private sector in providing goods and services. Private firms, it is claimed, are relatively free of bureaucratic red tape and political maneuvering. In short, it is argued that private production is carried on at closer to minimum feasible cost than is public production and that therefore production should generally be left in private hands.

Whether government production of goods and services is in fact relatively inefficient might be debated. Incentives other than profit maximization might be found. Efficiency aside, however, there are two weaknesses in this argument. One is that it confuses production by the government with spending on public goods. Over half of federal government spending on goods and services is on goods produced by private firms; most of the rest consists of payment for services of government employees. In other words, for the most part, government is not in competition with private industry. Second, there is no use in showing that private producers are more efficient than government if private producers are unable or unwilling to provide the goods or services in question. This is the case in providing police and fire protection, defense, public health services, etc. In short, government spending on public goods is on goods the private sector would not supply or would not supply efficiently if it were allowed the resources to do so. To eliminate defense spending because it is wastefully administered and let people buy more cars instead resembles, as one observer put it, the action taken by "a man in Atlanta who wanted to go to New Orleans but decided to take the train to New York because it was faster."[10] This is not to say that we should be tolerant of waste in the administration of government programs. The lack of the profit incentive can make efficiency a serious problem. But if these programs are meeting public wants, as expressed through the political process, then demonstrating that there is waste in the program is an argument for eliminating waste, not for eliminating the programs.

Another argument states that the taxes necessary to raise funds to pay for government expenditures distort consumer and producer choices by causing the market prices of goods, as well as of the fac-

[10] Francis M. Bator, *The Question of Government Spending* (Harper and Row, 1960), p. 107.

tors of production, to diverge from what they would be in the absence of these taxes. This involves a "dead-weight" loss of efficiency in the production of private goods. Though "waste" engendered by the tax system may be real and significant, this is not an argument against federal spending. For if such expenditures were eliminated, the market economy would not itself provide the public goods or transfer payments. Taxes ought to be considered, as was mentioned earlier, in estimating the benefits and costs from government programs, but the existence of the cost of tax collection does not mean that the program is not worthwhile.

There are also some fallacies in the arguments commonly used to support more government spending. Quite often, for example, government expenditures are compared with GNP, and it is implied that in some sense a rise in government spending is justified by a rise in GNP, or that government spending *should* rise in step with GNP. While such a comparison may provide a measure of the relative importance of government in the economy, it is no criterion for judging government expenditures. They should be gauged as far as possible on the basis of costs and benefits to society. This may mean that at times government spending need not grow as fast as GNP or at other times that government spending should grow faster than GNP. Government spending relative to GNP by itself does not provide a useful criterion for evaluating expenditures.

It is also wrong to judge federal expenditures solely with reference to fiscal policy. When there is unemployment, there may be strong pressure for increased spending. But the programs involved in the spending must be judged on efficiency grounds also. There is usually no justification for "make work" spending just to solve unemployment. Tax cuts should be considered as an alternative, and where this is not feasible or is ineffective and increased spending is necessary for fiscal policy reasons, programs should be chosen in which the benefits exceed the costs. In short, more federal spending, even when there is unemployment, is not necessarily "good."

These examples of "rules of thumb" and the faulty reasoning behind each could be extended almost indefinitely. Statements like "when defense spending goes up, nondefense spending should go down by an equal amount," or "government spending is generally wasteful," reflect a misunderstanding of the function of government spending and taxation.

Summary

Federal government expenditures arise out of the public's desire for public and semi-public goods which are not provided at all, or are provided inadequately by the private market, and to achieve equity in the distribution of income. There are no precise rules or guidelines that define the proper amount of expenditure for each of these purposes. For some federal programs, such as water resource development, an estimate of costs and benefits of projects can be used to determine the proper amount of expenditure. In many cases, however, cost-benefit analysis cannot readily be applied to answer the question of how much the federal government should spend on various public goods or semi-public goods. In short, federal government expenditure policy turns largely on the citizenry's preferences for federal versus state-local responsibility, public versus private goods, and the distribution of income.

APPENDIXES

TABLE A-1. Federal Receipts from the Public, by Type, 1934–65[a]

(In millions of dollars)

Fiscal year	Individual income taxes	Corporation income taxes	Excise taxes	Employment taxes	Estate and gift taxes	Customs	Unemployment insurance deposits	Veterans' insurance premiums	Other	Total[b]
1934	410	393	1,691	—	110	299	—	66	157	3,126
1935	512	572	1,934	—	211	322	—	63	209	3,823
1936	666	746	1,693	—	376	371	19	64	219	4,154
1937	1,066	1,073	1,857	252	303	471	292	63	259	5,636
1938	1,287	1,328	1,864	714	413	342	748	63	281	7,040
1939	1,022	1,138	1,861	739	357	302	811	63	271	6,564
1940	959	1,123	1,937	836	357	331	860	60	380	6,879
1941	1,400	2,029	2,555	929	403	365	892	61	568	9,202
1942	3,205	4,727	3,393	1,191	421	369	1,096	102	600	15,104
1943	6,490	9,570	4,093	1,505	442	308	1,218	335	1,136	25,097
1944	19,701	14,737	4,761	1,747	507	417	1,349	836	3,763	47,818
1945	18,415	15,146	6,267	1,785	638	341	1,256	1,012	5,302	50,162
1946	16,157	11,833	6,999	1,707	669	424	1,010	903	3,835	43,537
1947	17,835	8,569	7,207	2,030	770	477	1,005	571	5,067	43,531
1948	19,305	9,678	7,356	2,388	890	403	1,007	434	3,895	45,357
1949	15,548	11,195	7,502	2,476	780	367	985	431	2,293	41,576
1950	15,745	10,448	7,549	2,881	698	407	1,098	440	1,673	40,940
1951	21,643	14,106	8,648	3,928	708	609	1,363	520	1,865	53,390
1952	27,913	21,225	8,851	4,563	818	533	1,439	473	2,197	68,013
1953	30,108	21,238	9,868	4,941	881	596	1,371	428	2,067	71,499
1954	29,542	21,101	9,945	5,382	934	542	1,246	426	2,508	71,626
1955	28,747	17,861	9,131	6,166	924	585	1,146	441	2,834	67,836
1956	32,188	20,880	9,929	7,228	1,161	682	1,330	441	3,249	77,087
1957	35,620	21,167	10,534	7,520	1,365	735	1,542	452	3,171	82,105
1958	34,724	20,074	10,638	8,565	1,393	782	1,501	485	3,730	81,892
1959	36,719	17,309	10,578	8,767	1,333	925	1,700	477	3,851	81,660
1960	40,715	21,494	11,676	11,067	1,606	1,105	2,167	482	4,766	95,078
1961	41,338	20,954	11,860	12,405	1,896	982	2,398	504	4,905	97,242
1962	45,571	20,523	12,534	12,561	2,016	1,142	2,729	501	4,288	101,865
1963	47,588	21,579	13,194	14,862	2,167	1,205	3,009	494	5,641	109,739
1964	48,647	23,493	13,731	16,832	2,394	1,252	3,042	494	5,596	115,530
1965[c]	47,000	25,600	14,372	16,685	2,800	1,415	2,950	494	6,068	117,384

Sources: U. S. Bureau of the Budget and Treasury Department.

[a] Receipts are net after refunds.

[b] Totals from 1934 through 1941 may not be precise to the level of significance shown because adjustments were for *major* intragovernmental transactions only.

[c] Estimates.

123

TABLE A-2. Federal Receipts from the Public, by Type, 1934–65

(As a percentage of total receipts)

Fiscal year	Individual income taxes	Corporation income taxes	Excise taxes	Employment taxes	Estate and gift taxes	Customs	Unemployment insurance deposits	Veterans' insurance premiums	Other	Total
1934	13.1	12.6	54.1	—	3.5	9.6	—	2.1	5.0	100.0
1935	13.4	15.0	50.6	—	5.5	8.4	—	1.6	5.5	100.0
1936	16.0	18.0	40.8	—	9.1	8.9	0.4	1.5	5.3	100.0
1937	18.9	19.0	32.9	4.5	5.4	8.4	5.2	1.1	4.6	100.0
1938	18.3	18.9	26.5	10.1	5.9	4.9	10.6	0.9	3.9	100.0
1939	15.5	17.3	28.4	11.3	5.4	4.6	12.4	1.0	4.1	100.0
1940	14.0	16.3	28.2	12.2	5.2	4.8	12.5	0.9	5.5	100.0
1941	15.2	22.0	27.8	10.1	4.4	3.9	9.7	0.7	6.2	100.0
1942	21.2	31.3	22.5	7.9	2.8	2.4	7.3	0.7	3.9	100.0
1943	25.8	38.1	16.3	6.0	1.8	1.2	5.0	1.3	4.5	100.0
1944	41.2	30.8	10.0	3.7	1.1	0.9	2.8	1.7	7.9	100.0
1945	36.7	30.2	12.5	3.6	1.3	0.6	2.5	2.0	10.6	100.0
1946	37.1	27.2	16.1	3.9	1.5	1.0	2.3	2.1	8.8	100.0
1947	40.9	19.7	16.6	4.7	1.8	1.1	2.3	1.3	11.6	100.0
1948	42.6	21.3	16.2	5.3	2.0	0.9	2.2	0.9	8.6	100.0
1949	37.4	26.9	18.0	6.0	1.9	0.9	2.4	1.0	5.5	100.0
1950	38.5	25.5	18.4	7.0	1.7	1.0	2.7	1.1	4.1	100.0
1951	40.5	26.4	16.2	7.4	1.3	1.1	2.6	1.0	3.5	100.0
1952	41.0	31.2	13.0	6.7	1.2	0.8	2.1	0.7	3.3	100.0
1953	42.1	29.7	13.8	6.9	1.2	0.8	2.0	0.6	2.9	100.0
1954	41.2	29.5	13.9	7.5	1.3	0.8	1.7	0.6	3.5	100.0
1955	42.4	26.3	13.5	9.1	1.4	0.8	1.7	0.7	4.1	100.0
1956	41.8	27.1	12.9	9.4	1.5	0.8	1.7	0.6	4.2	100.0
1957	43.4	25.8	12.8	9.2	1.7	0.9	1.9	0.5	3.8	100.0
1958	42.4	24.5	13.0	10.4	1.7	1.0	1.8	0.6	4.6	100.0
1959	45.0	21.2	13.0	10.7	1.6	1.1	2.1	0.6	4.7	100.0
1960	42.8	22.6	12.3	11.6	1.7	1.2	2.3	0.5	5.0	100.0
1961	42.5	21.5	12.2	12.8	1.9	1.0	2.5	0.5	5.1	100.0
1962	44.7	20.1	12.3	12.3	2.0	1.1	2.7	0.5	4.3	100.0
1963	43.4	19.7	12.0	13.5	2.0	1.1	2.7	0.5	5.1	100.0
1964	42.2	20.3	11.9	14.6	2.1	1.1	2.6	0.4	4.8	100.0
1965	40.0	21.8	12.2	14.2	2.4	1.2	2.5	0.4	5.2	100.0

Source: See Table A-1.

124

TABLE A-3. Federal Payments to the Public, by Function, 1948–65

(In millions of dollars)

Fiscal year	National defense	International affairs and finance[b]	Agriculture and agricultural resources	Veterans' benefits and services	Interest	Health, labor and welfare	Other	Total
1948	13,015	5,554	559	6,897	3,909	3,035	3,492	36,493
1949	13,097	6,232	2,537	7,032	3,977	3,860	3,835	40,570
1950	13,121	4,596	2,858	9,277	4,315	5,100	3,880	43,147
1951	22,649	3,795	656	6,050	4,134	4,866	3,647	45,797
1952	44,243	2,946	1,155	5,823	4,134	5,666	3,995	67,962
1953	50,586	2,217	2,967	4,953	4,706	6,544	4,796	76,769
1954	47,138	1,696	2,617	5,042	4,620	8,083	2,662	71,858
1955	40,852	2,044	4,399	5,114	4,664	9,485	3,979	70,537
1956	40,854	1,624	4,977	5,328	5,115	10,254	4,394	72,546
1957	43,442	2,637	4,627	5,448	5,266	12,108	6,478	80,006
1958	44,552	2,651	4,347	5,828	5,884	15,757	4,453	83,472
1959	46,673	2,398	7,052	5,910	5,350	18,017	9,352	94,752
1960	45,915	1,574	4,877	5,907	7,233	19,107	9,715	94,328
1961	47,685	2,153	5,183	6,187	7,257	22,364	8,713	99,542
1962	51,462	2,492	5,942	6,092	6,940	23,975	10,759	107,662
1963	53,429	2,242	7,266	5,971	7,427	25,698	11,718	113,751
1964	54,514	3,492	5,846	6,107	8,011	27,285	15,076	120,332
1965[a]	52,347	3,636	4,650	5,985	8,461	28,868	16,944	121,393

Source: U. S. Bureau of the Budget.
[a] Estimates.
[b] Beginning in 1964, expenditures under the Food for Peace program are included in International Affairs. Prior to that date, they were included in Agriculture.

TABLE A-4. Federal Payments to the Public, by Function, 1948–65

(As a percentage of total payments)

Fiscal year	National defense	Inter-national affairs and finance	Agriculture and agricultural resources	Veterans' benefits and services	Interest	Health, labor and welfare	Other
1948	35.6	15.2	1.5	18.9	10.7	8.4	9.6
1949	32.3	15.4	6.3	17.3	9.8	9.5	9.5
1950	30.4	10.7	6.6	21.5	10.0	11.8	9.0
1951	49.5	8.3	1.4	13.2	9.0	10.6	8.0
1952	65.1	4.3	1.7	8.6	6.1	8.3	5.9
1953	66.0	2.9	3.9	6.4	6.1	8.5	6.2
1954	65.6	2.4	3.6	7.1	6.4	11.2	3.7
1955	58.0	3.0	6.2	7.2	6.6	13.4	5.6
1956	56.3	2.2	7.0	7.3	7.0	14.1	6.1
1957	54.3	3.3	5.8	6.8	6.6	15.1	8.1
1958	53.4	3.2	5.2	7.0	7.0	18.9	5.3
1959	49.2	2.5	7.4	6.3	5.6	19.0	10.0
1960	48.6	1.6	5.2	6.3	7.7	20.3	10.3
1961	47.9	2.2	5.2	6.2	7.3	22.5	8.7
1962	47.8	2.3	5.5	5.7	6.4	22.3	10.0
1963	47.0	2.0	6.4	5.2	6.5	22.6	10.3
1964	45.3	2.9	4.9	5.1	6.7	22.7	12.5
1965	43.5	3.0	3.8	4.9	7.0	23.8	14.0

Source: See Table A-3. Percentages may not add to 100.0 due to rounding.

TABLE A-5. Federal Government Surpluses or Deficits in the Administrative Budget, the Cash Budget, and the National Income Accounts, 1932–65[a]

(In billions of dollars)

Fiscal years	Surplus (+) or Deficit (−)		
	Administrative budget	Cash budget	National income accounts
1932	− 2.7	− 2.8	− 1.5
1933	− 2.6	− 2.6	− 1.3
1934	− 3.6	− 3.4	− 2.9
1935	− 2.8	− 2.5	− 2.6
1936	− 4.4	− 3.4	− 3.5
1937	− 2.8	− 2.8	− 0.2
1938	− 1.8	− 0.2	− 2.0
1939	− 3.9	− 2.8	− 2.2
1940	− 3.9	− 2.7	− 1.4
1941	− 6.2	− 4.8	− 1.6
1942	−21.5	−19.4	−14.0
1943	−57.4	−53.8	−47.1
1944	−51.4	−46.1	−47.9
1945	−53.9	−45.0	−53.2
1946	−20.7	−18.2	−19.3
1947	+ 0.7	+ 7.1	+11.2
1948	+ 8.4	+ 8.9	+11.4
1949	− 1.8	+ 1.0	+ 0.2
1950	− 3.1	− 2.2	− 0.2
1951	+ 3.5	+ 7.6	+16.3
1952	− 4.0	c	− 1.1
1953	− 9.4	− 5.3	− 6.3
1954	− 3.1	− 0.2	− 8.6
1955	− 4.2	− 2.7	− 1.1
1956	+ 1.6	+ 4.5	+ 6.8
1957	+ 1.6	+ 2.1	+ 4.4
1958	− 2.8	− 1.6	− 4.9
1959	−12.4	−13.1	− 4.4
1960	+ 1.2	+ 0.8	+ 2.4
1961	− 3.9	− 2.3	− 2.4
1962	− 6.4	− 5.8	− 1.9
1963	− 6.3	− 4.0	− 2.8
1964	− 8.2	− 4.8	− 3.9
1965[b]	− 6.3	− 4.0	− 5.0

Source: U.S. Bureau of the Budget.
[a] Surpluses or deficits in the national income accounts for 1932–40 are for calendar years.
[b] Estimates.
[c] Less than $50 million.

TABLE A-6. Public Debt, Private Debt, and Interest on Public Debt in Relation to Gross National Product, 1929–64

(Dollar items in billions)

End of Year	Public Debt[b] Amount	Public Debt[b] Percentage of GNP	Interest on Public Debt Amount	Interest on Public Debt Percentage of GNP	Private Debt[c] Amount	Private Debt[c] Percentage of GNP
1929	16.3	16	0.7	0.7	161.2	154
1930	16.0	16	0.7	0.7	160.4	157
1931	17.8	23	0.7	0.9	147.9	194
1932	20.8	36	0.7	1.2	136.7	234
1933	24.0	43	0.8	1.4	127.5	228
1934	31.5	48	1.0	1.5	125.1	192
1935	35.1	48	1.0	1.4	124.2	171
1936	39.1	47	1.1	1.3	126.4	153
1937	41.9	46	1.2	1.3	126.7	140
1938	44.4	52	1.1	1.3	123.1	144
1939	47.6	52	1.2	1.3	124.3	136
1940	50.9	51	1.3	1.3	128.6	128
1941	64.3	51	1.4	1.1	139.0	110
1942	112.5	71	1.7	1.0	141.5	89
1943	170.1	88	2.5	1.3	144.3	75
1944	232.1	110	3.3	1.6	144.8	68
1945	278.7	130	4.3	2.0	139.9	65
1946	259.5	123	5.2	2.5	154.1	73
1947	257.0	110	5.2	2.2	179.7	77
1948	252.9	97	5.4	2.0	200.9	77
1949	257.2	100	5.6	2.2	211.7	82
1950	256.7	90	5.8	2.0	250.9	88
1951	259.5	79	6.0	1.8	282.2	86
1952	267.4	77	6.3	1.8	306.5	88
1953	275.2	75	6.6	1.8	329.8	90
1954	278.8	77	6.9	1.9	348.4	96
1955	280.8	71	6.9	1.7	402.5	101
1956	276.7	66	7.6	1.8	439.4	105
1957	275.0	62	8.4	1.9	467.8	106
1958	283.0	64	8.0	1.8	499.1	101
1959	290.9	60	9.2	1.9	547.4	113
1960	290.4	58	10.3	2.0	589.2	117
1961	296.5	57	9.9	1.9	633.3	122
1962	304.0	55	10.5	1.9	689.0	124
1963	310.1	53	11.1	1.9	752.8	129
1964[a]	318.7	51	11.5	1.8	810.9	130

Sources: Data for public and private debt are from the *Economic Report of the President* (1965), pp. 254, 260; data for interest on public debt for 1929–53 are from U. S. Department of Commerce, *National Income*, 1954 edition, pp. 172–73; for 1954–57, from *U. S. Income and Output* (1957), p. 164; for 1958–63, from *Survey of Current Business*, July 1960, July 1964, and May 1965 issues.

a Preliminary estimates.

b Gross federal debt and guaranteed issues.

c Net private debt outstanding.

TABLE A-7. Ownership of Public Debt, 1939–64

(Par values, in billions of dollars)[a]

End of year	Total public debt[b]	Held by U. S. Government investment accounts	Held by Federal Reserve banks	Privately Held						
				Total	Commercial banks	Mutual savings banks and insurance companies	Other corporations	State, local governments	Individuals	Miscellaneous
1939	47.6	6.5	2.5	38.6	15.9	9.4	2.2	.4	10.1	.7
1940	50.9	7.6	2.2	41.1	17.3	10.1	2.0	.5	10.6	.7
1941	64.3	9.5	2.3	52.5	21.4	11.9	4.0	.7	13.6	.9
1942	112.5	12.2	6.2	94.0	41.1	15.8	10.1	1.0	23.7	2.3
1943	170.1	16.9	11.5	141.6	59.9	21.2	16.4	2.1	37.6	4.4
1944	232.1	21.7	18.8	191.6	77.7	28.0	21.4	4.3	53.3	7.0
1945	278.7	27.0	24.3	227.4	90.8	34.7	22.2	6.5	64.1	9.1
1946	259.5	30.9	23.3	205.2	74.5	36.7	15.3	6.3	64.2	8.1
1947	257.0	34.4	22.6	200.1	68.7	35.9	14.1	7.3	65.7	8.4
1948	252.9	37.3	23.3	192.2	62.5	32.7	14.8	7.9	65.5	8.9
1949	257.2	39.4	18.9	198.9	66.8	31.5	16.8	8.1	66.3	9.4
1950	256.7	39.2	20.8	196.8	61.8	29.6	19.7	8.8	66.3	10.5
1951	259.5	42.3	23.8	193.4	61.6	26.3	20.7	9.6	64.6	10.6
1952	267.4	45.9	24.7	196.9	63.4	25.5	19.9	11.1	65.2	11.7
1953	275.2	48.3	25.9	201.0	63.7	25.1	21.5	12.7	64.8	13.2
1954	278.8	49.6	24.9	204.2	69.2	24.1	19.2	14.4	63.4	13.9
1955	280.8	51.7	24.8	204.3	62.0	23.1	23.5	15.3	64.7	15.6
1956	276.7	54.0	24.9	197.8	59.5	21.3	19.1	16.3	65.5	16.1
1957	275.0	55.2	24.2	195.5	59.5	20.2	18.6	16.6	64.0	16.6
1958	283.0	54.4	26.3	202.2	67.5	19.9	18.8	16.5	63.0	16.6
1959	290.9	53.7	26.6	210.6	60.3	19.5	22.8	18.0	68.0	22.1
1960	290.4	55.1	27.4	207.9	62.1	18.1	20.1	18.7	64.7	24.2
1961	296.5	54.5	28.9	213.1	67.2	17.5	20.0	19.0	64.4	25.0
1962	304.0	55.6	30.8	217.6	67.2	17.6	20.2	20.1	64.5	28.0
1963	310.1	58.1	33.6	218.5	64.3	17.1	20.6	21.1	66.2	29.2
1964[c]	318.7	60.6	37.0	221.1	63.5	16.8	19.7	22.2	68.0	31.1

Source: *Economic Report of the President* (1965), p. 256.
[a] United States savings bonds, series A–F and J, are included at current redemption value.
[b] Gross public debt and guaranteed issues.
[c] Preliminary estimates.

Bibliographical Notes

Chapter II. Types of Federal Budgets and Their Uses

Good general discussions and comparisons of the three types of federal budgets are provided in the following: "Budgets of the Federal Government," *Monthly Review of the Federal Reserve Bank of Saint Louis,* Vol. 44, No. 7, July 1962, pp. 9-12; *Economic Report of the President* (1962), pp. 77-78; and "Federal Receipts and Expenditures—Alternative Measures," *Monthly Review, Federal Reserve Bank of Kansas City,* August 1961, pp. 3-9.

For more detailed comparisons see U.S. Congress, Joint Economic Committee, *The Federal Budget As an Economic Document,* 87 Cong. 1 sess. (1962), Chapter 7; or the budget document itself, for example, U.S. Bureau of the Budget, *The Budget of the United States Government, Fiscal Year 1966, Special Analysis A* ("Three Measures of Federal Financial Transactions"), pp. 356-65.

A more thorough explanation of the national income accounts and the federal national income budget may be found in U.S. Department of Commerce, *National Income: A Supplement to the Survey of Current Business,* 1954 edition, Parts II and III; and in *U.S. Income and Output: A Supplement to the Survey of Current Business,* November 1958, Chapter 2.

There is considerable literature on the advantages and disadvantages of the budget concepts and suggested improvements. The May 1963 issue of *The Review of Economics and Statistics* (Harvard University Press) was devoted to federal budget concepts and includes articles by Francis M. Bator, Samuel M. Cohn, Gerhard Colm and Peter Wagner, Otto Eckstein, Richard Goode, George Jaszi, Richard A. Musgrave, Carl Shoup, and Stephen Taylor, Helmut Wendell, and Daniel Brill. See also Chamber of Commerce of the United States of America, *Report of the Committee for Improving the Federal Budget* (1962).

Chapter III. The Budget Process

The best general source of information on the budget process is Jesse Burkhead, *Government Budgeting,* New York: John Wiley and Sons, 1956, especially Chapters 4 and 10-14. There is a memorandum available from the U.S. Bureau of the Budget entitled "Preparation and Execution of the Federal Budget," which provides additional information on the federal budget cycle. Other good sources of general information are: U.S. Congress, Joint Economic Committee, *The Federal Budget As an Economic Document,* 87 Cong. 2 sess., 1962, Chapter 2; Arthur Smithies, *The Budgetary Process in the United States,* New York: McGraw-Hill, 1955; and Committee for Economic Development, *Control of Federal Government Expenditures,* January 1955.

Material on recent developments in federal budgeting is to be found in: U.S. Congress, Joint Economic Committee, Subcommittee on Economic Statistics, *The Federal Budget As an Economic Document,* Hearings, 88 Cong. 2 sess., 1963, pp. 149-212 (Testimony by Charles A. Schultze, Sam Cohn, and Carl Tiller, all of the U.S. Bureau of the Budget); U.S. Bureau of the Budget, "Improvements in Budget Presentation, 1947 to 1962," Staff Paper, August 1962; and Gerhard Colm, *The Federal Budget and the National Economy,* Washington: National Planning Association, Planning Statement No. 90, 1955.

Chapter IV. The Record: Federal Spending and Taxes

The best single source of data on the record of federal spending and taxation is the budget document itself. Every issue contains historical tables for the cash, administrative, and national income budgets. For example, the 1965 budget document contains a section of historical tables (pages 453-63) on the three kinds of budgets. For less detailed data covering a longer period, see U.S. Bureau of the Census, *Historical Statistics of the United States: Colonial Times to 1957,* Y 205-714. Readable summaries of federal fiscal history are: M. Slade Kendrick, *A Century and a Half of Federal Expenditures,* New York: National Bureau of Economic Research, 1955; Arnold M. Soloway, "The Growth of Government Over the Past Fifty Years: An Analytical Review," in U.S. Congress, Joint Economic Committee, *Federal Expenditure Policy for Economic Growth and Stability,* 85 Cong. 1 sess. (1957); and Paul B. Trescott, "Some Historical Aspects of Federal Fiscal Policy," in *ibid.*

Details not found in any of these sources are sometimes available on request from the U.S. Bureau of the Budget.

132 Federal Budget Policy

Chapter V. Federal Budget Policy and Economic Policy

The relation between planned spending and GNP is discussed more thoroughly in most basic economics textbooks. For example, see: Charles L. Schultze, *National Income Analysis,* Englewood Cliffs: Prentice-Hall, 1964; Daniel M. Hamberg, *Principles of a Growing Economy,* New York: W. W. Norton, 1961, Chapters 4-13; Lloyd Reynolds, *Economics: A General Introduction,* Homewood, Ill.: Richard D. Irwin, 1963, Chapters 18-19.

The effects of tax or expenditure changes on planned spending, output, prices, and employment are also discussed in most of these same sources. See Schultze, *op. cit.,* Chapter 3, pages 55-65; Hamberg, *op. cit.,* Chapters 12 and 17; and Reynolds, *op. cit.,* Chapter 20. A discussion of this may also be found in Otto Eckstein, *Public Finance,* Englewood Cliffs: Prentice-Hall, 1964, Chapter 7; and *Economic Report of the President,* 1963, pages 45-52.

A discussion of the problems involved in using tax or expenditure changes to affect the economy may be found in: Reynolds, *op. cit.,* Chapter 20; Eckstein, *op. cit.,* Chapter 7; Hamberg, *op. cit.,* Chapter 17; and Wilfred A. Lewis, *Federal Fiscal Policy in Postwar Recessions,* Washington: Brookings Institution, 1962, pages 17-24.

The concept of the "budget line" and "full employment surplus (or deficit)" is used in the *Economic Report of the President,* 1962, pages 78-81. It goes back to a 1947 publication of the Committee for Economic Development, *Taxes and the Budget,* and to statements by Charles Schultze, in *Current Economic Situation and Outlook,* U.S. Congress, Joint Economic Committee Hearings, 86 Cong. 2 sess., 1961, pages 120-22, and Herbert Stein, in U.S. Congress, Joint Economic Committee, Hearings on the *Economic Report of the President,* 87 Cong. 1 sess., 1961, pages 209ff. See also Lewis, *op. cit.,* pages 7-14.

The automatic fiscal stabilizers are discussed in the *Economic Report of the President,* 1963, pages 67-69, and Lewis, *op. cit.,* Chapters II and III.

Chapter VI. Fiscal Policy and the Budget Program

For general discussions of alternative budget policies, see: Arthur Smithies, *The Budgetary Process in the United States,* New York: McGraw-Hill, 1955, pages 437-69; Committee for Economic Development, *Taxes and the Budget: A Program for Prosperity in a Free Economy,* November 1947; Committee for Economic Development, *Fiscal and Monetary Policy for High Employment,* 1961; Milton Friedman, "A

Monetary and Fiscal Framework for Economic Stability," *American Economic Review,* June 1948, pages 245-64; and Gunnar Myrdal, "Fiscal Policy in the Business Cycle," *American Economic Review,* March 1939, pages 183-93.

For a discussion of the full employment surplus as a measure of fiscal action, see Robert Solomon, paper presented at the Annual Meeting of the American Statistical Association, Minneapolis, Minnesota, September 8, 1962. For an evaluation of the CED budget, see Walter W. Heller, "CED's Stabilizing Budget Policy After Ten Years," *American Economic Review,* September 1957, pages 634-51.

Chapter VII. Fiscal Policy and the National Debt

For general discussions of the national debt, its history, its characteristics, and the economics of the debt, the following are recommended: Marshall A. Robinson, *The National Debt Ceiling, an Experiment in Fiscal Policy,* Washington: Brookings Institution, 1959; Ansel M. Sharp and Bernard F. Sliger, *Public Finance,* Homewood, Ill.: Dorsey Press, 1964, pp. 161-88; and the *Economic Report of the President,* 1963, pp. 78-83.

For more technical treatments of the question of the burden of the debt, as well as other related issues, see: James M. Buchanan, *Public Principles of Public Debt,* Homewood, Ill.: Richard D. Irwin, 1958; Alvin H. Hansen, "The Federal Debt Reconsidered: A Review Article," *Review of Economics and Statistics,* November 1959, pp. 370-78; James E. Meade, "Is the National Debt a Burden?" *Oxford Economic Papers,* June 1958, pp. 163-83; Franco Modigliani, "Long-Run Implications of Alternative Fiscal Policies and the Burden of the National Debt," *Economic Journal,* December 1961, pp. 730-55; E. J. Mishan, "How to Make a Burden of the Public Debt," *Journal of Political Economy,* December 1963, pp. 529-42; Abba Lerner, "The Burden of the Debt," *Review of Economics and Statistics,* May 1961, pp. 139-41; and William G. Bowen, Richard G. Paris, and David H. Kopf, "The Public Debt: A Burden on Future Generations?" *American Economic Review,* September 1960, pp. 701-06.

Chapter VIII. Determining the Need for Federal Spending

For a general discussion on the need for federal spending, the following are recommended: Francis M. Bator, *The Question of Government Spending,* Harper and Row, 1960; Robert L. Heilbroner and Peter L.

Bernstein, *A Primer on Government Spending,* Alfred A. Knopf and Random House, 1963, Chapters 1-4; Gerhard Colm, "The Theory of Public Expenditures," in *Essays in Public Finance and Fiscal Policy,* Oxford University Press, 1955, pp. 27-48; and Walter W. Heller, "Economics and the Applied Theory of Public Expenditures," in U.S. Congress, Joint Economic Committee, *Federal Expenditures Policy for Economic Growth and Stability,* 85 Cong. 1 sess., pp. 72-100.

For a detailed discussion of the cost-benefit analysis as applied to federal spending, see: John F. Due, *Government Finance,* Homewood, Ill.: Richard D. Irwin, 1954, pp. 19-25; John V. Krutilla and Otto Eckstein, *Multiple-Purpose River Development,* Johns Hopkins Press, 1958; Otto Eckstein, *Water Resource Development,* Harvard University Press, 1958; Charles J. Hitch and Roland N. McKean, *The Economics of Defense in the Nuclear Age,* Harvard University Press, 1960; and Robert Dorfman, ed., *Measuring Benefits of Government Investments,* Washington, Brookings Institution, 1965.

Deriving the Cash Budget from the Administrative Budget

Adding Receipts and Expenditures of Trust Funds and Government-Sponsored Enterprises

The first step in deriving the cash budget from the administrative budget is to add in the receipts and expenditures of federally managed trust funds and government enterprises sponsored by the federal government.

There are over 150 trust and deposit funds managed by the federal government, but seven dominate in size of receipts and expenditures. These are: (1) the Federal old-age and survivors' insurance trust fund (generally thought of as the social security fund); (2) the federal disability insurance trust fund; (3) federal employees' retirement funds; (4) the railroad retirement fund; (5) the unemployment trust fund; (6) the veterans' life insurance trust fund; and (7) the highway trust fund.

Certain revenues are earmarked for each of these funds. Revenue of the OASI, DI, railroad retirement account, and federal employees' trust funds are largely from payroll taxes on employers, employees, and the self-employed. Employer taxes levied by the states and the federal government (for administrative expense and benefits) are credited to the unemployment trust fund. The highway trust fund is credited with the revenue from certain excises levied by the federal government on motor fuels, tires, innertubes, tread rubber, and trucks, and from vehicle use taxes. The funds also are credited with interest income from their investments. The excess of receipts over expenditures in any year is invested in special (usually nonmarketable) United States government securities, and many funds for which receipts were planned to exceed expenditures in their early years have accumulated substantial holdings of these securities and receive considerable interest income.

Most expenditures of the trust funds are not budgeted as are expenditures in the administrative budget. They consist largely of benefit payments to individuals, whose eligibility is prescribed by the laws establishing the trust fund.[1] For example, OASI is paid to those who apply, subject to certain eligibility criteria, such as a minimum earnings period, age, etc. In other cases, such as the highway trust fund, payments are made for a certain predefined activity (building certain types of highways), and the funds are committed in accordance with available tax revenue.

As has been pointed out, the trust funds invest their excess money in federal obligations. When receipts exceed payments, they buy securities; when payments exceed receipts, they cash in their government securities. In principle, the funds would be so regulated that over the long run, payments would not exceed receipts from taxes and interest income, but in practice the benefits have at times been increased without adjustment of taxes, so that particular funds may run prolonged deficits until earmarked taxes are increased.[2]

In the discussion of the administrative budget it was noted that, except for occasional payments of interest to, or purchases of securities by, the federal government, no account is taken of government-*sponsored* enterprise in that budget concept; whereas the operating results of government-*owned* enterprise are entered as net expenditure items. In deriving the cash budget, the net deficits or surpluses of government-sponsored enterprises are added in as a net expenditure.[3] This represents the net payment to the public by the government as a result of the activity of these enterprises; although they are not part of the budget process, their activity still represents federal activity. The estimated net deficits (or surpluses) of federal government-sponsored enterprises in the fiscal year 1965 are shown below (in millions of dollars)[4]:

[1] Note, however, that certain expenditures in the administrative budget are budgeted this way, for example, veterans' benefits.

[2] A deficit for an extended period for a particular fund does not necessarily mean that it is actuarially unsound. It is expected, for example, that the unemployment compensation trust fund will run deficits during periods of severe unemployment.

[3] The deficits or surpluses of government-sponsored enterprises are estimated by investment in United States securities and debt issuance, for which the Treasury acts as fiscal agent; amounts equal to the net debt issuance or net disinvestments of such enterprises are used as an estimate of net expenditures.

[4] Data are from U.S. Bureau of the Budget, *The Budget of the United States Government, Fiscal Year 1966*, p. 351.

Federal Deposit Insurance Corporation	−194
Federal Home Loan Banks	−250
Banks for Cooperatives	79
Federal Intermediate Credit Banks	208
Federal Land Banks	302
Total (net) expenditures	145

Table C-1 shows the receipts and expenditures of the trust funds and government-sponsored enterprises for fiscal 1965, by major fund and in the aggregate. The OASI, unemployment, and highway funds by themselves accounted for over $23 billion of the $29 billion dollars of expenditures and also for a similarly large proportion of receipts. As in the administrative budget, certain transactions between the various trust funds were deducted as "interfund transactions" from both receipts and expenditures in arriving at these totals.

TABLE C-1. Receipts and Expenditures of Federal Trust Funds and Government-Sponsored Expenditures, Fiscal Year 1965

(In millions of dollars, estimated)[a]

Item	Receipts	Expenditures	Excess of receipts over expenditures
Federal Old-Age and Survivors Insurance trust fund	16,162	15,966	196
Federal Disability trust fund	1,222	1,518	−296
Unemployment trust fund	4,013	3,336	677
Railroad Retirement account	1,289	1,185	104
Federal Employees retirement funds	2,670	1,380	1,290
Highway trust funds	3,649	4,101	−452
Veterans' Life Insurance trust fund	713	632	81
Federal National Mortgage Association	—	48	− 48
Other trust funds	1,376	1,361	15
Deposit funds	—	− 47	47
Interfund transactions	−579	−579	0
Subtotal	30,515	28,901	1,614
Government-sponsored enterprises	—	145	−145
Total	30,515	29,045	1,469

Source: *1966 Budget*, p. 370.
[a] Details may not add to totals due to rounding.

Intragovernmental Transactions

Interfund transactions have already been subtracted from receipts and expenditures in the administrative budget and trust fund accounts taken separately. There are, however, certain transactions between the trust funds and the administrative budget accounts that must also be eliminated. That is, if we are measuring cash payments to, and receipts from, the nonfederal public, we eliminate payments and receipts *within* the federal government, that is, between trust funds and operating agencies. There are administrative budget receipts that are also trust fund expenditures and administrative budget expenditures that are also trust fund receipts. The detail of these items is shown in Table C-2. In fiscal year 1965 they totaled $4,234 million.

Debt Issuance in Lieu of Checks

In certain instances the federal government makes expenditures by issuing bonds or notes or by increasing the value of bonds outstanding, instead of by issuing checks. These expenditures are counted in the ad-

TABLE C-2. Intragovernmental Transactions Excluded from the Consolidated Cash Totals, Fiscal Year 1965

(In millions of dollars, estimated)[a]

1. Administrative budget receipts that are trust fund expenditures	
Franchise taxes from government-sponsored enterprises	5
Dividends, interest, etc. from FNMA	16
Reimbursements for expenses and services	67
Repayment of advances	103
Total	191
2. Trust fund receipts that are administrative budget expenditures	
Interest on investments of trust funds	1,747
Contributions for military service credits	14
Payments to the District of Columbia	111
Payments to employee retirement funds	1,104
Payments to Indian tribal funds	20
Advances to unemployment trust fund	. . .
Contributions to veterans life insurance funds	6
Other	1
Total	3,003
3. Deductions from employees' salaries for retirement	1,039
Total, intragovernmental transactions (1+2+3)	4,234

Source: *1966 Budget*, p. 360.
[a] Details may not add to totals due to rounding.

TABLE C-3. Debt Issuance in Lieu of Checks, Fiscal Year 1965

(In millions of dollars, estimated)

Accrued interest added to the value of debt (savings bonds)	833
Treasury notes issued for:	
International Monetary Fund	250
International Development Association	−5
Inter-American Development Bank	—
United Nations funds securities	42
Armed forces leave bonds issued	−1
Adjusted service bonds issued	a
Excess profits tax refund bonds issued	a
Total, debt issuance in lieu of checks, net	1,119

Source: *1966 Budget*, p. 361.
a Less than $0.5 million.

ministrative budget when the debt is issued or increased, even though no cash outflow occurs until the debt is redeemed for cash. Since the cash budget seeks to measure *cash* expenditures, these expenditures must not be included until the debt is redeemed, that is, until a cash outflow takes place. This is what the adjustment entitled "Debt issuance in lieu of checks" in Table 2, Chapter II, accomplishes. For example, interest payments on savings bonds are on an accrual basis in the administrative budget. In the cash budget, this interest is recorded only when the bonds are cashed, and the adjustment then accounts for the difference between the amount of interest accrued and the amount paid.

Another example is the issuance of noninterest-bearing notes by the United States to the International Monetary Fund, the International Development Association, and the Inter-American Development Bank, in payment of part of the United States subscription to the capital of these agencies. These are treated as expenditures in the administrative budget when the debt is issued, but they are not considered as expenditures in the cash budget until the notes are redeemed for cash. The adjustment "Debt issuance in lieu of checks" puts these expenditures on a cash basis.[5]

For fiscal year 1965, this adjustment is $1,119 million, as is shown in Table C-3.

Changes in Outstanding Checks

Another adjustment to put budget expenditures on a cash basis is to present expenditures in terms of "checks cashed." Administrative budget expenditures are in terms of "checks issued" by the government in paying its bills. If we seek a measure of payments to the public, this must

[5] For a discussion of this adjustment, see *1966 Budget*, pp. 360-61.

be converted to a "checks cashed" basis. (See Table 2 in Chapter II, "Changes in outstanding checks.")

Exercise of Monetary Authority

This deduction from administrative budget receipts in order to arrive at cash receipts from the public is made because the item is not a *cash* receipt from the public. It consists mostly of profits made by the federal government on the minting and disbursement of coin, that is, the difference between the cost of the metallic content of the coin plus minting costs, on the one hand, and the actual value of the coin as money on the other. Since this receipt is not a cash receipt from the public, it is deducted from administrative budget receipts.

Deriving the National Income Budget From the Cash Budget

As has been noted, the national income budget differs from the cash budget with respect to: (1) coverage, (2) netting and consolidation, (3) timing of receipts and expenditures, and (4) the exclusion of capital transactions. The first two types of adjustment have been discussed fully in Chapter II, so the discussion here relates to (3) and (4).

Differences in Timing

Timing adjustments are of considerable importance in the national income budget. The administrative and cash budgets record receipts as collected. The national income budget records business income taxes as they accrue or become a liability, even though the actual payment follows with a lag of about six months. Personal income taxes are recorded on a payment basis, that is, when individuals make quarterly or monthly payments to the government. Business receipts are generally put on an accrual basis and individual income taxes on a payments basis on the assumption that their impact on business and individuals occurs at time of accrual for business and time of payment for individuals.

Expenditures are adjusted for timing in several ways. First, purchases of goods and services are recorded as of the delivery date, although cash payment may precede or follow this. For wages paid to federal employees, cash payment is lagged only slightly behind services performed, so the difference is inconsequential. For goods purchased from the private sector, however, in many instances the difference is far greater.[1] Second,

[1] It should be noted that there are good reasons for questioning the use of "goods delivered" as a measure of the economic impact, in any given period, of federal purchases of goods. Generally the economic impact of federal spending for goods occurs long before the goods are actually delivered, in the form of private production activity and payments for labor, raw materials, etc. For elaboration of this

an adjustment is made for nonrecourse loans by banks and other private lenders that are guaranteed by the Commodity Credit Corporation, the federal agency which makes and guarantees loans on farm crops under the price support programs. These are not included in the cash budget as an expenditure until they are taken over by the CCC (although CCC *direct* loans are included as expenditures when made), and the government makes payment for them. However, the farmers usually expect the collateral to be forfeited and normally consider the bank loan as income. Hence the crops are effectively delivered when the private loan is extended, and therefore, an adjustment has to be made for this in the national income budget. Third, interest on savings bonds and Treasury bills is treated on an accrual basis (reversing the adjustment made in the cash budget) because whether paid out or not, this interest presumably has an impact on individuals and institutions when accrued. Finally, an adjustment also has to be made for certain foreign-currency transactions of the Commodity Credit Corporation. The CCC facilitates exports of surplus agricultural commodities by paying exporters dollars and accepting foreign currencies in payment. The cash budget includes this as an expenditure when dollar outlay occurs, whereas the national income account counts it when the subsequent expenditure (abroad) of the foreign currency takes place.

Exclusion of Capital Transactions

A number of so-called capital transactions are excluded from federal expenditures in the national income budget. These are generally federal loans or loan repayments and purchases and sales of existing physical assets, such as land, buildings, etc. Federal loans (or their repayment) do not represent federal purchases of output; they only enable the recipients to do so (or reduce their ability to do so in the case of repayment), and federal purchases of existing physical assets, such as buildings, do not represent purchases of current output but exchanges of assets, which are excluded from the national income accounts altogether.

---

point, see Murray Weidenbaum, "The Federal Government Spending Process," in U.S. Congress, Joint Economic Committee, *Federal Expenditure Policy for Economic Growth and Stability,* 85 Cong. 1 sess., Committee print (1957), pp. 493-506.

Index

Accrual accounting: in the national income accounts budget, 60n; and program budgeting, 34

Administrative budget, 2, 4-8, 14-15, 40n; for fiscal 1965, 6-7; items excluded from, 8; preparation of, 16-23; purpose of, 6, 14-15; relation to cash budget, 9-10, 14-15, 32

Administrative lag: in federal purchases of privately produced goods, 30; between recognition and action, 71

Agricultural benefit payments (*see also* Subsidies), 19, 29, 45, 47

Agriculture, federal spending on, 47, 115; as percentage of total federal expenditures, 109, 112

Agriculture, Department of: program budgeting in, 34

Allotment, by organizational unit, 28-29

Annually balanced budget. *See under* Budget policy.

Appeals on budget decisions, 17, 21, 22, 23, 27

Apportionment of obligational authority, 28-29, 30, 71

Appropriations (*see also under* Budget process), 16, 20, 22, 25, 26, 71; conference committee on in Congress, 27-28; coordination of decisions on, 36-37; defined, 23-24; initiation of legislation, 26, 26n; no-year, 24; Omnibus Appropriation Act, 35; one-year, 24; Presidential action on, 28

Audit of accounts, 2, 6, 16, 31; commercial audit, 31; comprehensive audit, 31; general audit, 31

Authorization (*see also under* Budget process), 16, 19-20, 23-28

Automatic fiscal stabilizers, 73-76, 79, 80, 83, 86, 88, 89

Automatic stabilizing budget proposals, 2; Committee for Economic Development proposal, 85-86; Friedman proposal, 86; Myrdal proposal, 86; weaknesses in, 86-88, 89

Balanced budget (*see also* Deficits; Surpluses), 2, 83-84, 86, 87

Bankruptcy, public: and the national debt, 3, 91, 92, 104-05, 106; *vs.* private, 84

Bator, Francis M., 118n

Bell, David, E., 29n

Berlin crisis: effect of on federal spending, 53n, 87

Budget and Accounting Act (1921), 5, 6

Budget call. *See under* Budget process.

Budget, federal (*see also* Budget policy; Budget process; Expenditures, federal; Receipts, federal; Revenues, federal; Taxes, federal): automatic fiscal stabilizers in, 73-76, 79, 80, 83, 86, 88, 89; congressional consideration of (*see* Congress); execution of, 28-31; forecasts involved in, 51; history of, 1, 2, 5-6, 39-53; impact of on economy, 1, 2, 5, 9, 15, 32, 33, 37, 38, 54-70, 76-78, 80, 89, 108, 119; improvements in document, 32-33; three concepts of (*see* Administrative budget;

143

Date Due

DEMCO NO 295

OCT 18				
MAY 12 '66				
MAY 23 '66 CANISIUS				